THE PRIVATE LIFE OF HENRY VIII

Few monarchs have had a private life so public as Henry VIII's. History and contemporary gossip have busied themselves with colorful stories of his six wives. As a result, he became the first sovereign to be looked on by succeeding generations as a dynamic person, not just a name.

In this new biography, N. Brysson Morrison reveals Henry's private life with an intimacy, ease, and immediacy that make the King's court live again. Along with Henry's magnificence of person and dress, his grandiose schemes, his affability and belligerence, she portrays each of his wives in her own right, exploring the differences in their backgrounds, personalities, and fates. It is a brilliant picture of a time, a man, and the women who loved him.

"This is a superb biography . . ."
—*Columbus Dispatch*

"Ruefully haunting . . . distinguished and evocative . . ." —*Spokane Daily Chronicle*

"Vivid . . ." —*Chicago Tribune*

ABOUT THE AUTHOR

N. BRYSSON MORRISON is eminently qualified to write of the private life of Henry VIII. Not only is she an experienced biographer (her MARY, QUEEN OF SCOTS was a Literary Guild selection and was chosen by Orville Prescott, of *The New York Times,* as one of his ten favorite books of the year), but she is a distinguished novelist as well, with all the insight and perception that make her characters so alive. THE PRIVATE LIFE OF HENRY VIII is her fifteenth work.

Miss Morrison is a born-and-bred Scotswoman who can trace her ancestry back to the time of William of Orange. It was then that the Huguenot "Brysson" of her name settled and married in Scotland. "The Lord," he wrote in his memoirs, "trysted me with a godly wife who bore me nine pleasant children."

Miss Morrison still lives in Scotland and does all her writing there, deep in the countryside. She interrupts her work for riding and walking and for her great love, the theater.

The
Private
Life Of
Henry VIII

N. Brysson Morrison

PAPERBACK LIBRARY

NEW YORK

PAPERBACK LIBRARY EDITION

First Printing: January, 1972
Second Printing: March, 1972
Third Printing: April, 1972

Cover portrait of Henry VIII by Hans Holbein. Galleria Nazionale d'Arte Antica, Rome. Scala, New York/Florence.

Library of Congress Catalogue Card Number: 63-13796

This Paperback Library Edition is published by arrangement with The Vanguard Press, Inc.

Paperback Library is a division of Coronet Communications, Inc. Its trademark, consisting of the words "Paperback Library" accompanied by an open book, is registered in the United States Patent Office. *Coronet Communications, Inc., 315 Park Avenue South, New York, N.Y. 10010.*

To

SIR GEORGE MIDDLETON, K.C.V.O.

Physician and Friend

*Their story . . . abides everywhere . . .
woven into the stuff of other men's lives.*

Contents

CHAPTER ONE

THE SMALL COLOSSUS

"Our King, he is the rose so red,
    That now does flourish fresh and gay:
Confound his foes, Lord, we beseech,
    And love His Grace both night and day!"

HE WAS born, this second son and third child, on the 28th June, 1491, and something of the shine and splendour of summer at its zenith accompanied him throughout his fifty-five years of life. Even his baby face with its broad brow and robust cheeks looked as though the sun were full upon it, and his hair when it began to grow was seen to gloss his head with gold. He was christened Henry after his father, the founder of the House of Tudor, but it was principally from his mother's side that he inherited his handsome looks.

Since the child is father to the man he, big for his age from infancy, prefigured he would grow more than life size. He stood sturdily, his legs apart, a small colossus equally distributing his weight. He had not been premature like his delicate brother but exuberant with health, learning with precocious ease, quick at mathematics, mastering

Latin, picking up their language from his French tutors as they taught him to write in a script that was a mixture of the new simple Italian style and the old-fashioned involved English.

A second son, no crown or throne awaited him as they awaited his brother Arthur, so he was destined for the Church, which meant he was grounded and educated to fill high clerical office. From his earliest days he loved music and had his own band of minstrels to delight him, quite apart from those of his kingly father or Prince Arthur. He loved not only to listen to music but to play it, and learnt the lute, organ and harpsichord until he had the skill of the master—not only to play it but to create it, so that in the days to come his songs and instrumental pieces soar amongst the finest productions of his times.

Honours were heaped on him before he was a year old. The baby cradled by his nurse Ann Luke was appointed Warden of the Cinque Ports and Constable of Dover Castle, received the honourable office of Earl Marshal, was created Duke of York, dubbed a Knight of the Bath, made Warden of the Scottish Marches, that turbulent neighbour over the border, so grievous a thorn in England's side, and invested with the Garter. Thus his painstaking father, by appropriating for his children great offices of state, channelled their fees, emoluments, perquisites, tributes, into the royal coffers. Better to keep high administrative posts in the family, under his direct supervision, than grant them to nobles who could become mischievous with power.

His children never noticed their father's thin hair and careworn face, and his subjects were unaware he was neither handsome nor distinguished. To his children, the King was their father, and he was the first sovereign in England to be referred to by his subjects as His Majesty.

He had the countenance of an ascetic, long-faced and pale, yet his thin tight mouth could twitch unexpectedly into a smile and his grey eyes suddenly quicken that shrewd hard face. He walked the earth carefully, as befitted one who had been captive or fugitive since the age of five until he had knelt on the ground of Bosworth Moor to thank God for giving him victory in battle. They had carried the plundered naked body of the defeated king from the field and placed his battered crown, found hidden in a hawthorn bush, on the head of the Welshman who had little hereditary right to it, while his victorious army, half the size of that it had vanquished, sang the *Te Deum*.

He had prayed that day for grace to rule in justice and in peace the people God, by giving him victory, had committed and assigned to him, and they were content to be governed by his resolute hand. For thirty years their country had been laid waste as two Houses warred for the crown. The ding-dong of battle had favoured now the white rose of York, now the red rose of Lancaster, and the impoverished land had shuddered to its roots while the long-drawn-out contest waged. It mattered little to his subjects that the man who now sat on the throne was there because his royal Lancaster grandmother had had a clandestine union with her Welsh clerk of the wardrobe. He grasped the sceptre with a strong hand, was establishing peace within the realm, and with peace came prosperity to the people.

No more disputed successions now a Prince of Wales was born to inherit from his father. Little wonder that his subjects called his consort "the good Queen", providing the royal nurseries with princes and princesses in goodly number. Her two young brothers had been murdered by the king her husband had defeated, and there were those who said she, Elizabeth of York, a king's daughter, had better right to the crown than her husband. But England had never been ruled by a queen, and they prayed God never would be. On the 22nd August, 1485, within an hour, the Welshman had won victory, crown and bride. His people needed no surer sign that Providence had arranged the union of their sovereign with Elizabeth of York when they flocked in their hundreds to see what had never been seen before: red and white roses, the rival colours of York and Lancaster, miraculously produced by the one bush.

On the rare occasions they saw her, borne in her litter or barge from castle to palace, they noticed more the gems that encrusted her coif than the face it framed. But to her children she was as heavenly-looking as an angel, fair-skinned, her hair pale gold banded on her smooth brow, her face still with a serenity that made it shine even when she did not smile.

The colourful feasts of Easter, Pentecost and Christmas lit the year with mirth and gaiety that followed the solemn religious services. Both the parents were devout, and the court stirred with divines, scholars and poets. Skelton, one of Prince Henry's teachers, was poet and priest; neither of his royal patrons could have been aware of his immorality, or read the coarsest of his satires. Christenings and birthdays, any family event that called for rejoicing, were celebrated with feasting and revelry. Favourite Greenwich House, the palace at Richmond, stately Westminster linked to the heart of London by the artery of the River Thames, towering Windsor—all were home to the royal children: parkland, hunting forest, gilded ceilings, costly tapestries, rich clothing, processions and pageantry the order of their common day.

Babies came and went in the royal nurseries, their lives a short passage from christening to catafalque, but the three eldest, Arthur, Margaret and Henry, survived the shocks of early infancy, as did Mary, a younger girl. Garbed in miniature adult clothes, they held their receptions with a majesty that was not make-believe. Each had his own household, which circled round him like constellations round the sun. This tended to separate members of a family one from another, yet their very uniqueness drew them together in bonds that were as taken for granted as the air they breathed.

Prince Arthur as eldest and heir was naturally the brightest luminary in these nursery days, the centre of the most brilliant galaxy. Henry never thought to envy or covet his brother's position, for that would mean to call in question the immutable decree of omnipotent God.

The extreme fairness of the heir to the throne enchanted the dark Spanish ambassadors when they were shown him as a lively baby with a view to his marriage with their Infanta. That was a betrothal upon which the father of the prospective bridegroom had set his heart. The Infanta's parents, King of Aragon and Queen of Castile, were wealthy, which meant the bride's dowry would be substantial. They were powerful, and England had need of a strong ally with France lying across a strip of water, ruled by a king who dreamed of making himself not only sovereign of England but of the world. Also such a glittering match would consolidate and add prestige to his position at home, with impostors and pretenders rising in the unlikeliest places to claim the throne in the Yorkist cause. But all was going well; little Katherine of Aragon was now betrothed by proxy to Prince Arthur, who was so far ahead with his Latin that soon he could write love letters to her learned highness since she could speak no English as he could speak no Spanish.

A sister Margaret divided the two brothers. Like all her parents' children, she received an advanced education; unlike them, it availed her not one whit. Headstrong and dominant, she was too like her younger brother for them to pull together when they grew up, but she supplied something the delicate Arthur lacked, and meant much to him.

Mary was to be Henry's favourite sister, the prettiest little thing imaginable, with sportive winning ways, but his life was too full to feel the need of her companionship. He had his strenuous male comrades to hunt with and tilt against, chief amongst whom was Charles Brandon, some years his senior. King Henry had him brought up with his younger son in memory of the boy's father who had saved his life at the expense of his own. To Mary, big Charles Brandon, from the humble ranks of the county gentry, was to become the knight of knights.

All the royal children were blond and had bright colouring, and Mary was to grow in beauty until she became the loveliest woman of her day. There is a portrait of the three eldest which shows them sitting at a plain table with two apples and three cherries. Prince Arthur is in the middle, as is proper for the eldest, his fair curls covered by a flat hat, a handsome child with an uncaptivating expression. Henry, on his right, might be a grown woman, his hair frizzed into tight wig-like curls. Margaret is the pleasantest of the trio, a little Eve in ermine sleeves, smiling as she grasps one of the two apples. All three, being so fair, have been depicted without lashes, which gives their eyes the round look of a sea-bird's.

All the children are shown as plump. The food in their century was strong and stimulating, the only drink to be had alcoholic, tea and coffee as yet unknown. Sugar or honey was taken with everything, even with roast meat, and the sweetmeats which followed a meal were its most important part and called the banquet. Even the English commons fed well on light-coloured bread and beer and quantities of meat, unlike the half-starved French peasantry. Such a diet tended to make a people swift on the draw with both tongue and hand. There were no half measures where their passions were concerned.

And the royal children had the best of everything. In Henry's case, the rich food, the strong meats, the heady wines and sweet cakes, the herbs, fruits and vegetables, went into what country folk call "a good skin". He was not

14

puffy like his elder brother but grew strong-boned and straight, self-reliant, smooth of skin and steady of eye, working off his energies learning to shoot and wrestle and cast the bar.

He was the guest of London when he was seven, the year his sister Mary was born. In anticipation of his visit, the civic authorities turned all vagabonds and anyone suffering from infectious disease out of the city. The unpocked citizens gave him a rousing welcome and the Mayor, on their behalf, presented him with a pair of gilt goblets, promising as he made the presentation of this "little and poor" gift, to remember him with a better one at some future time. On his part, the self-possessed young Prince made a charming speech, thanking Father Mayor and his Brethren for their great and kind remembrance of him which he trusted in time coming to deserve.

He saw them then, his father's subjects, lining the streets to watch him go by, the women as rough and full of animal spirits as the men. And there tossed like communication between these Londoners and him, the cynosure of their gaze, the shared excitement of the moment—they the beholders, he the beholden.

The subjects their father ruled were a lusty folk, who came of healthy stock, bold, hardy and keen to do business. With the stability of the new reign, trade increased and their far-sighted King negotiated a favourable commercial treaty with the Netherlands. Instead of shipping wool to feed foreign looms, the cloth itself was now woven in England and exported, and the clothier flourished where the weaver had waxed and waned.

They gathered to watch hangings and floggings, shouldering each other for a better view, feeding their eyes on spectacles such as a royal progress, at one with the clamour of life that filled street and market-place; but not quite at one with the ecclesiastical processions that wended to or from cathedral or abbey. They were unaware of that themselves as they stood there looking on with speculative eyes. It was not the crucifix, the crosier, the canopy they were to deride; it was the men who bore them, "Pope's men".

The assiduous columns of figures, each initialled by the royal H, were mounting into a fortune of millions. The greying face that bent over them had begun to age perceptibly, as though his forty-odd years had soured on him. He looked like a nut whose shell has shrivelled instead of decayed, and now enclosed no seeds to release. Always pious, his devotion became more intensified. It was rumoured he had consulted a soothsayer who warned him his life was in danger.

One grim November day his subjects learnt that the young Earl of Warwick, royal Yorkist and best qualified pretender to the throne, had been executed for treason. As the Tower, where he had been incarcerated at the age of ten, had been his home since Bosworth, his opportunities for treason were few and far between; but that he had been allowed to grow to manhood proved that the first Tudor king preferred imprisoning his competitors to murdering them. His execution now was said to be at the instigation of Ferdinand and Isabella of Spain, who did not wish their daughter to marry the Prince of Wales if one day he might be deposed by a rival.

The over-sanguine Spanish ambassador assured his master and mistress that his death left not a doubtful drop of royal blood in the kingdom, but many years later the sensitive bride was to remember her marriage had been sealed by the spilling of innocent blood.

She sailed from her sunny home of myrtles and pomegranates in the spring, arriving in England that blustering October with her retinue of prelates, governess—for she was only sixteen, a year older than her groom—duenna, donnas and grandees. But her welcome at Plymouth made up for the inhospitable weather. The Spaniards noted to their satisfaction that she could not have been received with greater rejoicings if she had been the Saviour of the world.

She was brought towards London in easy stages, the nobility and gentry of the counties she passed through entertaining her on her way. Her arrival in England had the effect of a stone splashed into a pool, causing currents that swirled across the whole country. Each destination she reached on her way swelled more waves and ripples, so that as she neared London accompanied by a train of four hundred English knights and gentlemen, all mounted and dressed in scarlet and black, she and the capital became like the vortex.

Some of the difficulty of travelling and communication can be gauged when we learn it was not until a month after her arrival that the King himself set out with the bridegroom to greet his daughter-in-law. It was now November, and pelting rain made the going hard over bad roads.

Young Henry learnt before the news percolated throughout the court that Spanish cavaliers had sent forward a message stipulating their Infanta could not be seen by either her bridegroom or his father until her wedding day. The English King's reply had the force of an ultimatum: as the Spanish Infanta was now in the heart of the realm of which he was master, he might look at her if he so desired.

And he did so desire, for his suspicions were thoroughly aroused that a so-called Spanish custom was a pretext to cloak some deformity of the bride. He arrived in his wet riding-clothes at the entrance of her apartment, where a Spanish archbishop, a bishop and a count blocked his entry. Every English heart beat higher when it was known what short shrift was made of their protestations as they were brusquely informed that even if she were in her bed, he meant to see and speak with her.

17

There was nothing wrong with the Infanta. She could understand neither her father-in-law nor her groom as they could not understand her, but so courteous in their own language was each to the other, so great the pleasure had they in what they saw, that the air was gladdened with welcome.

She entered the city by London Bridge, one of the wonders of the world with its span of nineteen arches and white pillars. To the approaching traveller, London presented a forest-like picture, with branching masts and rigging of the vessels on its river, countless spires rising above the huddle of roofs, and garden trees spreading their leafless limbs like ship tackle. On that November day every bell rang out clamorous and jubilant, vying with the citizenry who, man, woman and child, roared their welcome at the bride from across the seas.

Young Henry was her escort and rode at her right side. His sister-in-law had come as a surprise to him. He knew his father was greatly taken not only with her appearance but her manners, which were so beautiful they made her beautiful. Here was someone who could not be other than she appeared, like a well-strung instrument that could only play in tune. But she was not dark as one imagined a Spaniard would be; instead her hair was a rich auburn, and she was fair-skinned as either Margaret or Mary. Her lively face lit and kindled in response to all she saw around her.

She rode a mule after the fashion of Spain, sitting on it on what looked like a small arm-chair. She wore a broad round hat tied under her chin with lace of gold to keep it on her head in that wild English weather. Under it was a coif of carnation colour and her copper hair streamed over her shoulders.

Her face eager as she looked at them, the Londoners took her to their hearts the moment they saw her, bellowing their appreciation as though loudness would convey to her what might be unintelligible in words. This was she who had come from far-away Spain to make her home amongst them, to wed their Prince and bear his sons and so make secure for ever the throne of England.

That was the young Duke of York, Prince Henry, who rode on her right side—a big lad with his bold brow for one not much older than ten, a prince every inch of him. They had a good laugh at the Spanish ladies-in-waiting who followed their mistress, each riding a mule as she did, each led by an English maid-of-honour on a palfrey. But the Spanish women did not sit on the same side as the English, so that each pair rode back to back and looked as though they were quarrelling.

This was the wedding of their Prince, the hope of England, taking place in the heart of their city, and they who witnessed it were the pulse of London. They saw Prince Arthur on his wedding day, clothed in white satin, endow his bride at the great door of St. Paul's Cathedral with one-third of his property. The bride was all in white too, her face half veiled with the outlandish foreign head-dress she wore. Prince Henry led her to the bishop's palace where the nuptial dinner was to take place in the grand banqueting-hall: it was said the gold plate she would eat from was embedded with precious stones and pearls and worth twenty thousand pounds.

The people were there a few days later at Westminster Hall where a tilt had been set up from the west gate to King Street. There they could feast their eyes on a stage hung with cloth of gold where the King and his lords sat on one side, and the Queen, the bride and their ladies on the other. There was no end to the sights to be seen, and when the tilting began the enthusiasm reached its peak as a wager-loving nation shouted its encouragement or howled its rating.

That night, in winter dark, the lurking streets were restless with people slipping past one another, featureless and without bulk until a torch flared, when faces leapt into being and a tangle of shadows separated into bodies. The King's palace of Westminster rode the darkness like some fantastic ship, an impression confirmed by the river on whose bank it stood.

Inside all was magnificence, splendour and majesty, feasting and cheer. The treasure of solid gold plate was on show, a sight to dazzle any Spaniard's eyes. Tapestry, arras and cloth of gold hid walls green with river damp and age. Trumpet notes, song and music lent the permanence of eternity to the passing moment.

The bridegroom sat at his father's right hand on the royal dais, with the nobility ranged in their degrees. At the King's left sat the Queen, the bride, princesses and ladies. This division of the sexes made it appear as though the packs of many cards had been shuffled with the kings all arranged on one side and the queens on the other.

Prince Henry watched his brother and their aunt dance together a stately figure before the company. He saw the bride and one of her ladies leave the dais. They wore their strange hooped Spanish dresses never before seen in England, which as they performed a slow and gliding movement swayed from their waists like bells. Now it was his turn.

He took his sister Margaret by the hand and together they danced two dances, quick and nimble, smiling to each other as they spun and whirled. They made an enchanting pair: the boy tall as his elder sister, strong, gallant and gay; she bright-haired, bright-faced at being the centre of attention.

So delighted were the King and Queen and the assembled company at their display that they took the floor once more. But finding his robe interfered with the leaping and cavorting of the dance, the young prince suddenly threw it aside and finished the figure in his jacket.

Already he had learnt to trip to his own measure.

CHAPTER TWO

THE KING IS DEAD

"The earth goeth on the earth glistring like gold,
The earth goes to earth sooner than it wold.
The earth builds on the earth castles and towers.
The earth says to the earth, 'All shall be ours'."

KING HENRY did not look to the English peerage for brides or grooms for his children: for one thing, there were few of the old aristocracy left after thirty despoiling years of the Roses War. He had surrounded himself with new men whose blood was anything but blue, lawyers and churchmen he could pay with judgeships and bishoprics instead of with grants of land. He accumulated and amassed; least of all did not part with land, bringing back to the crown estates that had passed to subjects, and adding to them the wide domains of his beaten opponents.

His children were royal, and royalty was a caste apart; it must marry royalty. His belief in marriage as an insurance of political union was implicit. Thus his son Henry and his small daughter Mary were proposed as the groom and bride of Eleanor, the granddaughter, and Charles, the grandson, of Ferdinand and Isabella. Charles was barely a year old but already King Henry had his eye on one who, heir to Castile and Aragon, Burgundy and Austria, grasped in his baby fist the political sceptre of Caesar.

Twice, when she was an infant, the hand of his eldest daughter Margaret was offered to James IV of Scotland. Surely such a marriage would stop for all time these running battles on the open seas between English and Scots captains, each calling the other pirate, these invasions over the borders from Scotland and costly incursions in retaliation from the English side, the harbouring and honouring of pretenders to the King of England's throne by his Scottish counterpart.

James was some fourteen years older than the child her father proposed as his bride, a handsome man with the Stewart red hair, a passionate lover and so nimble he could leap on his horse without touching his stirrup. His ambition was to marry a Spanish princess, and it was not until Ferdinand and Isabella told him they had no more single daughters that Scots ambassadors were sent over the border to discuss the marriage of their Stewart king with the Tudor princess.

They arrived for the betrothal, or engagement, ceremony not long after the bells of London had rung out the wedding of the Infanta and the Prince of Wales. Even hardheaded Scots could not wring from King Henry any more than a miserly dowry for his daughter, which the prospective bridegroom disdained to haggle over, and the twelve-year-old Margaret, his favourite child, signed in her square handwriting the marriage contract, binding herself to marry the right Excellent, right High and Mighty Prince James, King of Scotland.

She was called Queen of Scotland when she plighted her troth, but her father had stipulated he would not send her north for a further eighteen months. The ceremony, and jousting and ballets to celebrate it, took place at

Richmond where the King had erected a new palace from a burnt-out old one. It was a favourite place of his which he had renamed Richmond after his own name before he was crowned. Standing on a hill-top, it commanded a view so far flung that one felt the whole of England was pent within one's sight, that the whole of England was arched by a high blue sky below which the shining Thames wound between green meadows, dipping sunny uplands and woodlands that feathered the landscape.

All Margaret's family were at her betrothment and took part in the gaieties except her favourite brother, the Prince of Wales. Soon after their marriage King Henry had dispatched his son and bride to Ludlow Castle in Shropshire to keep court, govern the principality of Wales and live as man and wife. This was against the advice of his council: the bride was only sixteen, the bridegroom little more than fifteen.

Neither could speak the other's language; what converse they held together had to be in stilted Latin, and there does not appear to have been any mutual attraction between the youthful pair, or any degree of familiarity in a marriage that was doomed not to survive six months of growing pains. To the day of her death Katherine contended that her union with Arthur, Prince of Wales, had never been consummated.

Some historians state that he died of a decline, other of the plague prevalent that wet spring in the Ludlow district. His health had always been precarious and the bright colouring which betokened robust good health in his brother Henry was probably in him the sign of consumption. He had time to make his will, leaving all his personal property, jewels, plate and wearing apparel to his sister Margaret. His bride of less than six months is not mentioned.

The dire news was broken to the King by his confessor. It was the Queen who sustained him, summoning up all the comfort she could from her deep fount of religion, reminding him he had been an only child, yet God had ever preserved him and brought him where he was now. "God is where He was," she told him, "and we are both young." But at the memory of her best beloved child, her heart fainted within her: together husband and wife took their "painful sorrows".

Young Henry now found himself heir apparent at the age of ten, the focus of his grave father's solicitude, the centre of ever-increasing attention as he grew to potent manhood in exact ratio as his parent's years diminished.

Everything was different now. Beamed on him was the hope of a nation. God in His unsearchable wisdom had cut off Arthur in his prime and decreed Henry should take his place. Their father was God's anointed and ruled only by His grace, the crown could not be separated from the cross. That was why the *mystique* between subject and monarch was much the same as the *mystique* between worshipper and deity.

Henry felt it, although he was his father's son. Children of those days paid their parents unquestioning unremitting obedience; it was not the tribe with which their roots were bound, it was the family. And King Henry was not only his father, he was his sovereign.

The boy's mind did not choose to vault into the future, when he might be called upon to fill not a brother's but a parent's place. To let such a thought flicker across his mind was like blasphemy, but he grew up in the certain knowledge that when and if that time did come it would be by God's edict and God's alone.

He saw his sister-in-law when his mother sent for the young widow to come to her. Katherine's entry into London could not have been more different from her bridal triumph so short a time ago. Now she was boxed in a vehicle like a hearse covered with black, a widow who had lost both potential and actual position, amongst strangers whose language she neither spoke nor understood.

She wore her auburn hair smooth, parted in the centre above a face alive with intelligence. He would see her serious gaze upon him. Both knew her parents were negotiating for a marriage between them, but the prospect of a boy more than six years her junior as a husband cannot have appealed to her. Nevertheless what her father bade her, she would do.

A dispensation for a woman to marry her deceased husband's brother would be necessary, but the Pope would be only too willing to provide what a powerful prince asked. King Henry received the suggestion coldly. What touched him to the quick was the question of Katherine's dowry. Only part of the vast sum had been paid, and the wily Ferdinand, now his daughter was a widow, not only refused to pay any more but demanded the refund of his previous instalments. He met his match, however, in the tenacious King of England.

Chaffering and bargaining ceased if only temporarily when death stalked again into the royal household. Some ten months after her son, the mother died. On Candlemas Day, when good weather foretold a long winter and a bad crop and ill weather was lucky, Queen Elizabeth bore her seventh child, a daughter. She died unexpectedly nine days later on her birthday, and her baby did not long survive her.

Her death made a hole in the lives of all her children. It was not only they had lost their mother; an angel had departed and left them. The heavens were never quite the same when a star one had thought was fixed in its course was blotted out, never to reappear.

The King, always a solitary figure, retired by himself to nurse his grief. Something went out of his life at his consort's death; unconsciously he had walked in her light,

26

and when that was snuffed, what was unlovely and unamiable in his character was revealed.

He gave her a magnificent funeral, as though these thousands of torches, these crosses of white damask and of gold, mourning-hoods, tapers and cloth of majesty were in some dumb way to make up to one he had always kept carefully in the background, to avoid all appearance of ruling by her right.

When the eighteen months were spent he said good-bye to his elder daughter Margaret, giving her a prayer handbook on which he wrote, "Pray for your loving fader, that gave you thys book, and I gyve you at all tymes God's blessyng and myne. Henry R." Margaret's husband was the handsomest sovereign in Europe, who treated his small bride with the gentleness and consideration of an elder brother. Nevertheless she wrote home pettedly, in her atrocious handwriting, referring slightingly to her husband as "this King here" and lamenting she was not with her father.

Alive to the matrimonial, political and dowry advantages of a Spanish match, King Henry now proposed to marry his daughter-in-law himself, which so shocked her mother she commanded him to return Katherine straightway to Spain. Katherine's reaction to such a union was instantaneous: from that moment there was never any confidence between her and her father-in-law. He did not send her to Spain as her mother demanded, and when her father reduced his terms, agreed for a marriage treaty to be signed between his second son Henry and his first son's widow.

At the age of twelve young Henry was betrothed with great solemnity to his sister-in-law. The actual marriage was to take place two years later when he came of age at fourteen. The betrothal ceremony was performed in the Bishop of Salisbury's house in Fleet Street—it was December, not long after Katherine had celebrated her eighteenth birthday, although celebrate was not quite the word to use for a landmark she reached in an existence that was a kind of hiatus while she waited for her fate to be decided for her. Through the vacillating eight years that followed she never knew whether she was widow or bride. Certainly she felt more the first than the second, subjected as she was to every deprivation by her shrewd father-in-law while he argued with her parent over the terms of her portion.

The Archbishop of Canterbury, the highest church dignitary in England, opposed the mariage as absolutely unlawful. Did not the law of Moses forbid a man to take his brother's wife, calling it an unclean thing, and warning those who broke the law they would be childless? There were other prelates, however, who countered Leviticus with Deuteronomy, where a man was actually enjoined as his duty to take his dead brother's wife and raise seed. All that was needed to smooth away any difficulties was the Pope's dispensation which was tardy in coming and arrived after the betrothment, just in time to comfort Katherine's mother on her death-bed.

It was a new Pope who sat on St. Peter's throne in Rome, a swarthy buccaneer of a pontiff, and his dispensation did little to allay the Archbishop's scruples. He doubted very much whether it or the documents accompanying it were valid, and so influenced old Henry that young Henry found himself, on his coming of age when his marriage to Katherine was to take place, making formal protest that the contract between them was null and void. The occasion was all the more impressive because it was secret.

King Henry thus enhanced his son's value as a negotiable asset on the marriage market which the father had entered himself. There were other as, if not more, desirable brides than Katherine of Aragon for Henry minor, and more than one provocative prospect for Henry major.

28

Also Charles was no longer a baby and had another grandfather as well as Ferdinand, the Emperor Maximilian, with whom King Henry could scheme and bargain, using his child Mary as premium. No longer was he the subservient partner in any alliance with the King of Aragon. Now he was his rival.

His patience was rewarded at long last by the signing of a treaty of marriage between the ten-year-old Princess Mary and the eight-year-old Charles. With characteristic caution he demanded surety for the adequate dowry he paid to the Emperor Maximilian, and Princess Mary received a cluster of magnificent diamonds of the first water valued at twice that sum. Parsimonious by nature, her father was careful even after he had accrued great wealth, but he had ever known what became him as a king, and on an occasion such as this the entertainment of the foreign dignitaries and ambassadors was sumptuous and without parallel.

From this union would stem not only political but commercial benefits to the country he had long served as father-king. Perhaps he was aware that this was the last of his worldly triumphs as he sat there in the seat he could not share and from which only death would make him abdicate, a little apart from it all, a ghost at his own feast, just beyond the pale of the sun. He had after all turned the half century, but it was not years that had broken and bowed his health. For over two decades his rule had brought order out of chaos, peace in the place of arms, profit, not loss. He was leaving his son a consolidated kingdom, an undisputed title and an overflowing treasury.

His son and heir—his eye gladdened every time it rested upon him. All that was best in his ancestors made splendid the figure of young Henry, now approaching his eighteenth year. Tall as his royal grandfather, Edward IV, he inherited his handsomeness from him and his maternal grandmother. There was no one his match for prowess

29

at the athletic pursuits of his day; yet the hands that could draw a bow, tame a steed and shiver a lance could play the flute and virginals, write songs and ballads and set them to music. His love of learning and of the fine arts was a direct legacy from his father, and he had, because of the fortune of his birth and upbringing and person, what his father could never claim, the magnetism that attracts popularity.

In the few short months granted King Henry, tentative spring loosened the grip of winter. Turned in upon himself, the dying man began to settle his account with God by writing off men's liabilities. He issued pardons, and paid the fees of prisoners thrown into gaol for debt. This was not the violent death of his predecessors, but a withdrawal in good order from the field of action. Not a horse-trampled battle-ground but a hushed room in his beloved palace at Richmond. When his eyes closed for the last time, he knew the crown would not be thrown into the cockpit of civil war but would pass without division to the son kneeling at his bedside.

With his failing breath he commended to his heir his faithful counsellors. He adjured him to complete his marriage with Katherine, to defend the Church and make war on the infidel. Thus he died, the first and the greatest of the Tudors, leaving his wasted body in the big bed. Perhaps his most fitting epitaph were five words of the contemporary historian: "What he minded he compassed."

They bore him between hedges and trees pricked with spring green and bright with blossom. In London the cortège was met by the mayor and aldermen, not clad in their violet gowns but clothed in black from head to foot, to accompany to his final resting-place the King who had always paid back his debts to them in full and in record time.

From St. Paul's to Westminster the procession wended down the Strand, through streets lined with members of companies and crafts, to rest in the soaring vaulted chapel with its matchless altar, the crowning glory of the buildings the dead man had raised. There he was laid beside his queen, dwelling "more richly dead than he did alive in Richmond or any of his palaces".

As the coffin was lowered into the vault, the heralds took their tabards from their shoulders, hung them on the railing round the catafalque and lamented, "The noble King Henry the Seventh is dead!" Then they put their tabards on again and with one voice shouted the cry loud with joy, "Long live the noble King Henry the Eighth!" The new reign had begun.

CHAPTER THREE

LONG LIVE THE KING

"Pastime with good company
I love and shall until I die.
Grudge who will, but none deny,
So God be pleased this life will I
For my pastime,
Hunt, sing, and dance,
My heart is set;
All goodly sport
To my comfort
Who shall me let?"
—*Henry VIII*

THE new reign burst upon the country with the force of explosion when the people woke up to find they had not only a new king but a young one. There was a feeling of release, a quickening, the stimulus of change, as though the long-tended soil had suddenly blossomed and burgeoned. This was not so much a new beginning as transformation. Carving lost its medieval stiffness and became floreate and free, garments were slashed to show contrasting colours that flaunted with the arrogance of youth, hats brave with feathers took the place of the old king's monk-like hood. Instead of sober formality, there was ebullience and the excitement of exaggeration. It was as though everything had burst into song.

No longer did distance separate sovereign from his subjects; yet when they saw their new king, and he delighted to be seen, he seemed to them like someone with the shine of heaven upon him, everything about him golden, without peer, standing head and shoulders above lesser men. Open-handed and liberal, his very presence seemed to spread largesse, so forthcoming was he, the embodiment of what the nation desired their prince and king to be, who would rule over them as they wanted to be ruled.

Yes, they were due a change; the old sovereign had reigned for close on twenty-four years, and even those who remembered him when he came to the throne did not remember him as young. There are some born old, and he was one of them; maybe it was his coming into the world after the death of his father had something to do with it. Enshrined in his own chapel, embalmed by stone, was a fitting place to think of him—and leave him. God would rest his soul, for he had been a good and devout man. So was his son devout. He heard Mass three times a day, but as well he could draw a bow with greater strength than any man in England.

When he sent to the block two of his father's tax-gatherers, his popularity was enhanced even more. The people did not reason that after all the two councillors were simply tools for carrying out the old king's policy; by the time the axe had fallen, the victims had received only their deserts, the memory of the King's father was not defaced, and he had proved himself a lover of justice and wisdom.

He was to marry the Infanta, she who had been Prince Arthur's bride. Scarcely had the stir of the old king's funeral settled when the news was made public. It was common talk that the father in his death agony had urged his son to fulfil the marriage treaty. And it was only right that he should. Eight years if it was a day since she had sailed from far-away Spain to marry their prince, and now he was dead, she deserved King Henry after her long wake. There were some who spoke behind their hands, saying it was not right to marry your brother's widow, but royalty was a law unto itself or it wouldn't be royalty, and a good man like old King Henry would never have told his son to do what was wrong. He must have known that both Prince Arthur and his bride were so young when they married and they had so short a time to be abed before he died, it was not like a marriage at all.

The people only heard about the wedding after it had taken place on Barnaby Bright day in June, so early in the morning no one was afoot, privately in Greenwich Palace. It had to be private because their king who could do no wrong was still in mourning. The whole of London knew before the day was spent that the bride had been clad all in white to show she was a virgin. When they spoke about it amongst themselves, they told each other that hadn't they said so all along.

They saw her first as their Queen not a fortnight later when she and the King progressed in state to Westminster to be crowned. The streets of London were hung with tapestry for the occasion; Cornhill always did better than anywhere else and displayed cloth of gold.

Carried in a golden litter swung between white palfreys, there was not another woman in the realm to hold a candle to Katherine of Aragon, which was as it should be when she was bride and queen of such a king. Again the people marked she was clad in bridal white. The summer light made the jewelled crown on her head flash and glow, but nothing could eclipse her great beauty which was her long auburn hair that fell gloriously down her back, like a cloak above her embroidered white satin gown.

In the Abbey, when the people were asked if they would have Henry as their king, their "Yea, yea!" fierce with exultation sounded like the surge of oceans. They were witnesses of the festivities that followed, watched the goings to and fro of King and Queen. Never had they seen a groom more happy in and proud of his bride than their young lion of a king. This was no marriage he had been puffed into by a father's dying wish, but one he made of his own free choice and rejoiced in for all the world to see. As for the bride, her love for him made her at one with the people. They knew how she felt and held jubilee with her, she who was a king's daughter, worthy to be consort of theirs, fit mother for the sons she would bear him and England.

Within six weeks of his father's funeral, Henry was married, eight years of vacillation brushed aside in fewer weeks. He loved Katherine as a young and vigorous man loves for the first time, and his joy in her increased daily as he found her not only loving but with an intelligence that matched his own. She taught him Spanish to add to his list of languages, and for the first time since she had arrived in her adopted country she put her mind to learn English. She wrote to her father, asking him to send the King her lord three steeds on which he had set his heart, one a jennet, the second a Neapolitan, the third a Sicilian. Henry gave her one of his most beloved possessions, his mother's missal, in which he wrote in French, "If your remembrance is according to *my* affection, I shall not be forgotten in your prayers, for I am yours, Henry R. for ever."

Katherine on her part found herself lifted from a

tedious anxiety-ridden existence, so poor she had to sell bracelets to buy a dress, to become the centre of a gay and lively court, every luxury at her fingertips. Married life was one continual feasting, music day and night, summer and winter. Henry was the leading spirit in all the romps and revels that made short the winter evenings, Katherine the audience so ready with her praise and to be surprised. Spanish women were not brought up to follow hawk and hound like her sisters-in-law, but she was always waiting for him on his return, and there was no one with whom he would rather be.

These glad free days, with husband and wife both joyous and festive, whose chief delight was to please and honour the other, spending lavishly the wealthy patrimony the old king had so carefully garnered and guarded. Time hummed by merrily in a round of good company. The days were not long enough for all the pastimes and pursuits to be crowded into them; the nights, in which to love your wife.

Henry at eighteen had grown to full manhood but he was little more than a highly educated boy. The iron of his will, character and powerful mind were still malleable with youth, and he was unaware of his strength other than physical. The older he grew the more remarkable he was to become. He kept his father's councillors around him, except for the two he was advised to sacrifice on the block, but he had more to divert him than the council table, and they came to the conclusion he cared only for the pleasures of his age.

His chief adviser was his wife's father, Ferdinand, King of Aragon, who had made Katherine his ambassador at her husband's court. Henry would certainly have been startled had he looked over his wife's shoulder when she wrote to her father, "These kingdoms of your highness are in great tranquillity," but there is no doubt that for the first few years of his reign he was subservient to the powerful Spanish King, as his father had been before him. Henry's antipathy, generated by centuries and shared by every Englishman, was directed against France. A hundred years of war had left England only Calais as its remaining foothold in that country, and little more than a strip of water divided them. In the tug-of-war for world domination that pulled between Spain and France, Henry was bound to throw England's might behind Spain.

The young King entered the arena of Europe like a knight entering the lists, bearing the standard of the Pope, the Vicar of Christ. Henry's religion was that of his parents, stoutly orthodox. His counterparts in the various nerve centres of power were all old enough to be his grandfather, campaigners seasoned in intrigue, weathered by years of cynical scheming, deceit as native to them as the air they breathed between lips that spoke of God. Ferdinand of Spain heard he was accused by a rival of cheating him twice. "He lies," he contradicted, "I cheated him three times." Louis XII of France was not so decrepit and worn out that he could not still turn a political somersault whenever it suited him, and that swarthy soldier of a Pope, arch prince of the church, marched in step with whichever side opportunism dictated.

Before the end of the year Henry was able to write to Ferdinand that Katherine was pregnant. Heaven indeed was blessing him. He saw that every care was taken of his wife and that she did not run any risks with her health, but at the end of January, after days and nights protracted by cruel labour, the seven-month baby was stillborn. The fact it was a daughter made its death easier for Henry to bear. Katherine wrote her father that the stillbirth was considered an evil omen in England, but that Henry took it cheerfully. She thanked God for having given her such a husband.

Her confessor noted that the King adored her, and she him. Shortly she was pregnant again and on the first day of the new year she bore a son.

Henry's cup of happiness was full to overflowing. In a crescendo of triumph the christening took place of the tiny son, a small wan thing to support so much magnificence. He was named Henry, and given the style Prince of Wales.

His father made a pilgrimage of Walsingham to thank God for His bounty, and an elaborate tourney was staged at Westminster to commemorate what was of such portent to both King and people.

Despite his sense of kingship, Henry was always approachable; and even when his dignity increased with the burden of years, never inaccessible. Today he was young and big with affability, father of a son and heir. He responded to the frenzy of joy with which the London citizens greeted him. This was as much their hour as his. And when they put out their dirty grasping hands to touch him, he did not recoil.

Bystanders were allowed into the royal palaces on special occasions, and a horde of them waited at the lower end of the great hall when the King and his lords appeared. He was dressed in purple satin, his garments encrusted with gold. A large man, his puffed garb made him appear enormous, and he had the effect on his audience, unaccustomed to such richness, of superabundance.

A delirium of adoration seized them. They pressed forward and began to pluck his clothes from the King, greedy to possess at least a particle of something he had worn. Like jackdaws, they fastened on his lords to strip them bare of their glittering ornaments, monograms of H and K in solid gold. The divested King, who sat down to the banquet that night in his doublets and drawers, treated it all as gaily as a game, advising his courtiers to do as he did, consider their losses as largesse to the commonalty.

Three days later the child was dead. God, who had given Henry and Katherine a son and heir, granted him only seven weeks of life.

CHAPTER FOUR

FIRST VICTORY

"O then we marched into the French land,
  With drums and trumpets so merrily;
And then bespoke the King of France,
  'Lo, yonder comes proud King Henry.'"

THE uproarious christening celebrations were stilled and silenced as the King's baby son was buried in Westminster Abbey at the cost of ten thousand pounds. The elaborate funeral was mocked by any traces of the festivity and gladness that had preceded it. So grief-stricken was the King, ambassadors dared not offer their condolences.

But Henry had all the resilience of a well-trimmed bow. He recovered his natural buoyancy long before Katherine regained her composure, persuading her at last not to take their loss so to heart, and to cease her lamentations. That she was always in his thoughts even when they were not together was revealed by the many times he was heard to remark, "This will please the Queen," and "The Queen must hear of this."

Court life swirled round them once more, Henry the heart of it, the momentum that sent the days spinning.

When he was not hunting, there was archery and tennis. When they were not singing, there was dancing, masques and comedies. He was the handsomest man in the country, well above the usual height, fair-skinned, bright-complexioned, the stamp of nobility upon his unlined brow. And the only thing he hated was to do anything he did not choose; so he did not do it, for after all he was king.

Members of his council, accustomed to the authority of his father, complained amongst themselves that the sovereign should be present when important decisions were made. Only one disagreed, with smiling urbanity. "Let the King hawk and hunt," he said, "and not intermeddle with old men's cares."

He was a newcomer to the council chamber but already he was listened to, for he spoke with the voice of the leader. A man of commanding height with quick perceptive sight, he gravitated towards the centre as by natural law, and filled every position he attained to the manner born. His grace of bearing and eloquent tongue betrayed no trace of the Ipswich butcher's son. He had reached where he had through his own wit, learning and indefatigability, and an instinct for influential patrons.

There was nothing of the parvenu about Thomas Wolsey. He had long ago outstripped his beginnings, and was at home amongst the great and noble. There was no precariousness in his foothold on the ladder: every rung he climbed was tested and made secure as a spring-board for the next ascent.

The priest who had become one of the King's chaplains in Henry VII's reign began to move about the court in Henry VIII's, accomplished and diligent in his self-imposed task to serve Church and State. His love of music and the arts made play of the years that stretched between him and his sovereign lord and lady; they met on common ground. Warmed by his discretion and compassion, the Queen turned to him as friend, and he would be seen kneeling before his young king in that manner characteristic of him, attentive and deferential, listening with his whole head.

Religion was a very real part of Henry's life, not a worn-out convention to which he paid lip service. He needed no urging from an ecclesiastic when he heard France was besieging the Pope. His mind and Wolsey's moved as one in this as in so much else. He wrote he was prepared to sacrifice goods, life and kingdom for the Vicar of Christ and the Church, and joined his father-in-law King Ferdinand in uniting against Spain's arch rival and England's ancestral enemy. War was declared on France.

He travelled to Southampton to speed his departing army on its great enterprise. It was setting out to fight not the infidel Turk but the Most Christian Louis, who was prepared to lay sacrilegious hands on His Holiness.

It was May, and the further south the cavalcade journeyed, the milder it became. As they approached the coast, sea-gulls flew up from the ground like a sheet being waved. The sight of ships always set Henry's heart dancing; these galleys with their beak-heads used for ramming, lofty galleons and sturdy galleases were his pride and passion; the flap of sail, the tug of rigging, the stir of departure, music in his ears.

The army was to take ship for Spain, where it was to be joined by King Ferdinand's in the concerted invasion of France. Henry wished he could have sailed with his men: he did not take kindly to being left behind. His boundless energy, his matchless health, urged him to be in the thick of the battle. And all he could do was wish his army God-speed as it embarked on its lofty crusade.

Katherine had now mastered the English language and could speak it fluently, but she never lost the attractive Spanish accent which made her most ordinary sentence sound charming. Together they and Wolsey waited throughout that summer for news of victory. God would surely prosper the high purpose of Spain and England banded in holy alliance to fight for the Supreme Head of His Church on earth.

By October news reached them there had been no battle and their troops, near to insubordination, were on the brink of embarking for home. Henry's wrath knew no bounds. He wrote to his father-in-law to stop the return of the army, telling him to cut every man's throat who dared to refuse obedience. But he was too late: already his dishonoured troops who had never fought were on the high seas, making for home. The first military expedition of Henry's reign had ended in ignominy and disaster.

Ferdinand's trickster mind excelled itself juggling with plausible reasons why his army had not reinforced that of his son-in-law's. Henry, with Katherine at his side, could not believe that her father was perfidious, unlike his men who had been on the spot. They knew Ferdinand had used the presence of his English allies on Spanish soil as a providential screen while he waged an independent war of his own not against France, but against Navarre. To conquer that independent kingdom had always been a pet scheme of his, for now all Spain beyond the Pyrenees was under his rule.

Throughout the torrid alien summer the untried English troops, forced to inactivity, had drunk Spanish wine as if it were home-brewed beer. Officers in the heat of the day had been heard to blame Wolsey, not the King, as the cause of all the mischief, calling it a war of his making. Autumn had added to the hazards of unhealthy inaction and dysentery decimated the ranks. What remained of Henry's army embarked for home.

Ferdinand, who in the past had urged his son-in-law to recover his lost possessions in France, began to counsel him to make peace with Louis. What could be better than that Henry should add his signature to the truce which had been arranged behind his back between the Spanish and French Kings? But England dare not do anything so craven: her honour had been dragged in the mire, and her King refused to let it lie there, the taunt of both friend and foe.

This time he would lead his army himself. No more costly expeditions to unfamiliar shores: Calais, England's remaining French possession, was to be the base for the invasion of France. Henry landed there one summer evening, and felt below his feet earth that had been flattened through the centuries by the tramp of English armies.

He was accompanied by the main body of his troops, and disembarked with his banner and guard of six hundred picked men. Nothing had been left undone to impress the French and soldiery. Every detail of his entourage had been planned by that prince of showmen, Thomas Wolsey, who had even chosen the shade of the satin for the King's doublet.

Priests and singers, secretaries and clerks, sewers, grooms and pages of the chamber were in the retinue; even the King's lutanist had not been forgotten or the Master of his Jewel-house. Fourteen magnificent horses for Henry's own use travelled with him, royal as their master in their coverings of gold and crimson velvet hung with precious bells. In all the wealth and colour of the pageantry only one muted note was struck when, in a plain cassock on an undecked mule, was seen to ride in priestly humility the King's Almoner, Thomas Wolsey.

They left Calais to join the spearhead of their army which had already advanced into French territory. A wooden house where he could lodge instead of bivouacking might follow Henry on fourteen wagons wherever he went, but he did not always take advantage of Wolsey's foresight. Heavy rains made the going arduous and one drenching night he refused to undress: instead, he rode about the camp encouraging the watch. "Now that we have suffered at the beginning," he cheered them, "fortune promises us better things, God willing." Never had his men known such a King as this, who called them comrades and joined his archers in archery practice, surpassing them all. When German mercenaries, who marched with the English troops, pillaged a church, their king promptly had three of them hanged.

Every courier who left the camp for England carried with him letters to the Queen from Wolsey and from the King, unless he was too preoccupied with war. He had made Katherine regent before he left home, a wise step although unusual because she was a woman, and her letters to him were full of the war she had on her hands.

What had happened before was happening again. Every Scots sovereign from Malcolm Canmore had made a point of invading England whenever his neighbour was either engaged in hostilities with France or confused with civil war. James IV of Scotland might be married to Henry's sister Margaret, he might be bound by treaty not to make war on England; nevertheless he behaved as his ancestors had done before him and prepared to lead an army over the border to aid his old ally France.

Katherine quietened her fears for her husband's safety by occupying herself with preparations to meet the invaders. She wrote she was horribly busy making standards, banners and badges. "My heart is very good to it," she penned in her quaint language. All Henry's subjects at home were very glad to be busy with the Scots too; they looked upon fighting with their neighbours over the border as a form of pastime.

Henry, besieging Therouanne in France, knew that England was threatened at her back door by bellicose Scotland. He had left Thomas Howard, Earl of Surrey, in charge of the retaining army at home. Howard was the

45

family name of the great Duke of Norfolk, known as the Jockey, who had lost his life fighting on the losing side at the Battle of Bosworth. His oldest son, Thomas, wounded and taken prisoner on the field, had been attainted by Henry VII.

The only master Thomas Howard could serve was the master who had stripped him of everything that made life worth the living. Only a king had been powerful enough to do it, only a king could reinstate him to his father's glory. He submitted to the victor of Bosworth Moor.

He watched the new men nearest to the young King, as he had watched them round the old one, upstarts every one of them, filling posts that by hereditary right belonged to the nobility. But Henry VII had deflowered the aristocracy: in the whole of England there was only one duke and one marquis left, and that one duke was not the Duke of Norfolk.

He saw the same men round Henry VIII now he was king. Not a nobleman's son was the young sovereign's boon companion, but a big, blustering blockhead like Charles Brandon, adept only with lance and sword and renouncing the women he married when he wanted to take another wife. The progeny of a simple esquire (scratch the esquire and you find the yeoman) had been created Viscount Lisle since his master's succession, one remove below an earl, which it had taken patient years for Thomas Norfolk to regain.

Charles Brandon was very close to the King in the campaign in France, for he was marshal of the army. It was not all active service, siege and strategy. There were charming interludes, as when the Emperor Maximilian arrived in person to serve as a private at a hundred crowns a day under the English banners, and his daughter, Margaret of Savoy, joined her father. To entertain her Henry played the gitteron, lute and cornet, and danced and jousted before her. He "excelled every one as much

in agility in breaking spears as in nobleness of stature".
So close was Charles Brandon to the King, he even made
suit to the emperor's daughter, when Henry obligingly
helped him out with his French.

The ogre Louis, who had threatened the whole of
Christendom only a short year ago, did not lead his men
in person. Instead he drove out of Paris in a carriage, and
the war in his country reached him like echoes and
reverberations against old ear-drums.

This impression of unreality hung over the whole
campaign. A large French force arrived to raise the siege
but at the sight of the English troops panic seized it and
the French cavalry wheeled their horses. Their trot broke
into a canter, the canter became full gallop. It was a
bloodless fray, with a roll of prisoners and no toll of dead,
and was referred to ironically by the French as the Battle
of the Spurs. Henry had the exhilarating experience of
chasing the routed army as long as his horse would go, and
of taking prisoner the noblest blood of France. He often
relived that afternoon: he was never to know its like again.

He made his triumphal entry into the first French town
captured by English arms since the days of Joan of Arc.
Tournay, the richest city north of Paris, was besieged.
Within a week it fell. The French towns were going down
before the English like Jericho before the chosen children
of Israel: God was on their side.

Word was brought him that the English had crushingly
defeated the Scots at Flodden and killed their king.
Katherine wrote with pardonable pride that this victory
was the greatest honour that could be, and worth more
than all the crown of France. She sent him a piece of the
King of Scotland's coat to make banners out of. She
wished she could have sent the King of Scots himself but
"our Englishmen would not suffer it". "It should have
been better for him to have been in peace than to have
this reward. All that God sendeth is for the best." Her

letter, in which she addressed him as My husband and My Henry, ends touchingly, "Your humble wife and true servant, Katherine." She asked him what Thomas Howard was to do with the dead King's body.

James IV had died like a king and a soldier, fighting to his last breath. That may be why Henry could feel regret for his vaulting brother-in-law. "He has paid," he said, "a heavier penalty for his perfidy than we would have wished." He wrote to the Pope for permission to bury him with royal honours in St. Paul's; papal permission was necessary as the Scots King had been excommunicated for breaking his treaty with England. It was granted, but the interment never took place; perhaps the magnanimity of victory wore thin, and no one knows what became of the Scots King's body, honourable with wounds.

For his victory at Flodden Field, the dukedom of Norfolk was restored to Thomas Howard. At the same time Charles Brandon was raised to spectacular heights when the dukedom of Suffolk was conferred on him by his friend the King.

It was impossible in the sixteenth century to victual an army on foreign soil during winter. The five summer months were the fighting ones and they had now passed. A triumphant Henry sailed for home with England's prestige higher than it had stood for a century, so high indeed that the Spanish King was said to be afraid of his son-in-law's ever-growing influence. Katherine believed her husband's success was all due to his zeal for religion. England was now a power to be reckoned with.

She had kept faith single-handed this year, but next year allies were essential, for wars were costly, and Henry VII's wealth was rapidly draining away with these inroads upon it. A treaty was drawn up binding Henry, Maximilian and Ferdinand to a combined invasion of France the following summer. At the same time the pledge for

Henry's sister Mary to marry Ferdinand and Maximilian's grandson Charles was renewed.

Mary was a spirited girl of fifteen in 1513, her beauty was exquisite and every foreign ambassador voted her the loveliest princess in Europe. It was agreed the marriage should take place next year when the bridegroom-to-be came of age at fourteen. Meanwhile he wrote to her signing himself "Your husband", and she tactfully sighed with love for him whenever she looked at his portrait in the presence of the Spanish ambassadors.

The King's arrival home was quite different from his departure. He landed quietly at Dover and rode at once post-haste to surprise the Queen when "there was such a loving meeting between them that everyone rejoiced who witnessed it".

He never saw the baby son born to Katherine shortly before his return; either it was stillborn or it died immediately after birth. No one would have known of its abbreviated existence had the Venetian ambassador not scented it out and reported it to the world.

CHAPTER FIVE

THE NEW RIVAL

"Cloth of gold, do not despise,
  Though thou hast wedded cloth of frieze.
Cloth of frieze, be not too bold,
  Though thou hast wedded cloth of gold."

AFTER the giddy flights of victory, the alighting; after the
stirring events of 1513, the disposing and maintaining.
The year 1514 was a year of backwash; the currents that
lapped it were far-reaching enough, nevertheless they
were backwash.

Scotland at England's back door demanded urgent attention with its new king an infant in Margaret's arms.
Henry claimed for himself the empty title "Protector of
Scotland", and left his sister to strengthen the English influence in her adopted country, uphill work with such a
nation, to whom independence was the breath of its
existence.

Every country had its secret service and paid agents—
priests, merchantmen and servants. No sooner had
Ferdinand signed the treaty binding him, Maximilian and
Henry to a joint invasion of France than his son-in-law

and Wolsey learnt through informers of his allies' treachery. Maximilian and Ferdinand had entered into a secret pact to make war on England whenever Henry should renew hostilities on France. But their subtlety and double-dealing were outmatched by Wolsey's, who could play them at their own game and score hands down.

A nuncio was dispatched to France to mediate a peace between young Henry and old Louis, lately bereft of his wife. Henry was no longer intimidated by the French King; it was the French King's turn to be fearful of Henry, and he was prepared to pay him a high price in the form of pensions for peaceful settlement.

Wolsey was not only dexterously manipulating the reins of government until he was handling everything about the King but he was the royal family's confessor, confidant and friend. The one-time chaplain collected three bishoprics in the same year, was angling for the cardinal's hat and would not stop short at St. Peter's throne. His appetite for titles and aggrandisement was insatiable, as though the more he gained, the more successfully he obliterated his beginnings. Prince of the Church, he began to build a palace for himself with rose-red walls, near enough London to be convenient, far enough removed to be safe when plague struck the city.

1514 was to be the year in which the long-convenanted marriage between Mary Tudor and Spanish Charles was to be fulfilled, not later than May as stipulated in a treaty not three months old. January, February, March, April passed with no sign of Maximilian's purpose to seal his grandson's betrothal of six years' standing. It was repeated in England that the potential bridegroom had been heard to remark he wanted a wife, not a mother, referring to Mary's two years' seniority.

When May came and went with no move made to keep his word, Maximilian's breach of promise was proclaimed to the world. Immediately negotiations were concluded for the marriage of the sixteen-year-old Mary Tudor, jilted by Charles, to the aged, newly widowed Louis, King of France.

It was a brilliant coup on Henry's and Wolsey's part. England, now on equal footing with France and Spain, by aligning herself to one, dangerously outweighed the other. The marriage of an English Princess to the French King would cement the peace between the two countries and was calculated to affect adversely Henry's father-in-law who had played so false with him. What would Ferdinand feel at the prospect of his grandson's rejected bride producing an heir to the French throne?

Certainly his lovely sister had no desire to marry a decrepit old man, even though he was King of France. Henry knew perfectly well she was in love with his favourite, Charles Brandon, recently elevated Duke of Suffolk, who, bold and masculine, played havoc with women's hearts. But after all the widower was old, and sickly into the bargain; Mary was not, by the laws of nature, being asked to undergo a life sentence. If she furthered Henry's plans with her first marriage, her brother undertook to allow her to marry whom she chose when it came to her second.

It was not a happy year for Katherine, for her husband, not surprisingly, visited on his wife the ill-faith and betrayal of her unscrupulous parent, even threatening to put her away. Spain was anathema in her adopted country. The Spanish ambassador felt in England like a bull at whom everyone threw darts, nor did he find an ally in the Spanish-born Queen who was more English than the English. As for the King, every time his father-in-law's name was mentioned, he behaved in the most offensive manner possible. The ambassador added with bitter prophecy that if the King of Spain did not put a bridle on this young colt it would soon become impossible to control him.

Meanwhile the young colt was informing with some truth an attentive Venetian envoy that the only ruler in the world who kept faith was himself. "Therefore," he said with royal unction, "God Almighty, who knows this, prospers my affairs." If Katherine had now completely identified herself with her husband and his subjects, her husband was in the process of identifying his Maker with himself. The time was to come when Henry was to take the place of God, but the transition was gradual and no one could say when it actually occurred.

The King and Queen and their court progressed to Dover to see Mary embark for France. The marriage of the young English princess to the senile French King shocked all Europe; and Europe, accustomed to the ways of her sovereign lords, was not easily shocked. Mary was to be escorted by the Duke of Norfolk, her chamberlain and household, attended by her governess (whom she and her sister Margaret had called Mother Guildford from their infant days), servants and ladies-in-waiting, highly born girls, one of the youngest of whom was a Mary Boleyn.

It was September, and it must have seemed to the unwilling bride that the very elements were conspiring to keep her in England, for storm after storm came blustering across the narrow Channel, making sailing impossible. In his strong towered castle, called the Key of England, Henry passed the days with his court waiting for the winds to subside. These storm-beaten wintry walls had stood high on the white cliff for so long they had become part of the landscape. From embrasure slit and crenelle he could sight the coast of France. The expanse and might of the ocean did not over-awe him: he wanted ships strong enough to ride the waves, however high. Already, since coming to the throne, he had built *Mary Rose* and *Peter Pomegranate,* and this very year the *Henry Grace de Dieu,* known colloquially as *The Great*

53

Harry, had been launched, a wonder man-of-war the like of which England had never seen before.

Not until October did the winds drop, when the bride and her attendants were roused before dawn to take advantage of the fairer weather. The leave-takings were painful: Henry might wear in his hat Mary's magnificent Spanish jewel given to her as surety for a marriage that had not after all taken place, but family ties were strong in the enclosed Tudor circle and he loved his sprightly young sister. He tried to comfort the weeping girl by painting a picture for her of a happy widowhood. She clung piteously to Katherine, who gave her the assurance and support of an older generation yet was bound up in all the gaieties and joyousness of a young court, as proud of Mary's beauty as though she were her mother.

Soon after the bride's arrival in France, distressed letters reached "My good Brother" and Wolsey, whom she addressed as "Mine own good Lord", for she looked upon him as her spiritual father. Would to God, she wrote, my Lord of York (Wolsey) had come with her in the place of Norfolk, for then she was sure she should not have been left as she now was—with no one of her own about her except two or three of her youngest ladies-in-waiting. All had been sent back to England by her royal spouse, the Duke of Norfolk weakly acquiescing. He had not put up a fight even for Mother Guildford. Mary wrote Wolsey she would rather lose the whole of France as lose her counsel. But the homely King Louis had taken the strongest aversion to Mother Guildford. He was astute enough to see that the Englishwoman with her officious stewardship of her royal ward would cause trouble in the French court. He felt sure the King, his good and loving brother Henry, would understand that Louis could not be merry with his wife if a strange woman was with her the whole time. Mary was told it was unsuitable for the Queen of

France to have anyone such as a governess dictating to one who should command.

Dispatches describing the wedding reached England from the Duke of Suffolk, for the man who loved Mary Tudor was appointed by Henry as one of his ambassadors to see her crowned. In the jousting that followed, the Englishman laid about him to such an extent that he shocked the hostess country and killed a French cavalier.

Much did the Parisians wonder at the beauty of their new Queen, tall as a nymph, sweet of face and manner, skin and hair very fair to their dark Gallic gaze. With her spring-like vitality the bride blossomed through all the elaborate ceremonies that welcomed her arrival and led up to the climax of the wedding and coronation; they sat on her elderly groom, who had attacks of gout, more heavily than the cares of state. But he was enchanted with his young bride and heaped on her jewels the like of which Mary, a king's daughter, had never seen before. He was, however, judicious in his giving, chuckling as he explained that she was not to have them all at once but at different times, that he might be repaid by as many thank-you kisses as possible.

Henry received a letter from his new brother-in-law telling him he could not sufficiently praise his wife, that daily he loved her more, honoured and held her dear. Mary came to believe she was better without Mother Guildford and settled down to life with her royal husband, doing her best to content him in every way. Certainly she changed one or two things to make them more English. The French, for instance, had the curious custom of dining at eight in the morning and the King was accustomed to retiring for the night at six in the evening. Mary altered his dinner hour to noon, and he stayed up with her until midnight, just like the English court. She could not understand why his doctors should shake their heads warningly over this so much more natural arrangement.

That November Katherine held once again a living son, bent to kiss his brow, but the baby was premature and died a day or two later. Some attributed its premature birth to her husband's harshness over her father's treachery, but there is little ground for such an assumption. It was Katherine's second pregnancy that year, sufficient reason for its weak hold on life, and Henry shared with her what was sorrow for them both.

That New Year's Day, because she was better, he staged a ballet to celebrate her recovery and to amuse her. As, dressed in cloth of silver and blue velvet, he performed by light of torches with Charles Brandon and six other dancers the intricate figures of the ballet, his brother-in-law in France, his Christian Majesty Louis, suddenly died, not three months after his wedding.

Wolsey was at once instructed to write to the young widow not to enter into any matrimonial engagement. The next marriage of the King's sister must not be dictated by the policy of France. Mary's reply was that she was not a child. The English ambassade dispatched to take charge of her and her considerable property included Charles Brandon, Duke of Suffolk, who, before he left, swore the ambassador's oath that he would not abuse his trust to the young Queen consigned to his care.

The envoys were also charged to renew the league with France's new King. He was a young man, two years younger than his English counterpart, and the moment he joined the most exclusive club of Europe, that of crowned heads, Henry scented competition.

"The King of France, is he as tall as I am?" he wanted to know, and was told they were of a height. "What sort of leg has he?" came the anxious demand. "Spare," came the welcome answer. Then he opened his doublet and placed his hand on his thigh. "Look here," he invited, "I have a good calf to my leg." On learning Francis wore a beard, not to be outdone, he allowed his own to grow. It grew in reddish, so with his golden beard he outshone the French King.

Thus began a mutual rivalry that was to last for over thirty rankling years. Francis I had the same tall, broad-shouldered figure of the athlete as Henry, with an oval handsome face where Henry's was round. The King of England, with his golden hair, fair skin and bright colouring, looked celestial as a seraph; the King of France, like the devil.

He was married to the Princess Claude, daughter of King Louis, whose fate of a libertine husband was that which does befall some virtuous women. Marriage did not deter him from making advances to the lovely English widow. Every day that passed in France seemed like a thousand to Mary, racked with toothache and unable to stop weeping. She wrote that she desired to return to her beloved brother, from whom she neved wanted to be parted again.

Never, Charles Brandon communicated to his kingly friend, had he seen a woman weep as she did. He discovered two English friars had visited her, telling her that if she left France she would never land in England, as the Duke of Suffolk had orders to take her to Flanders where she was to be given in marriage to the Prince who had rejected her, Charles of Spain. Rather than that fate, Mary told him, she would prefer to be torn in pieces.

Nothing her lover said would drive this fear from her mind. There was only one way he could prove he had not come to entice her to her doom and that was there and then to marry her himself. "So I granted thereto," he wrote, "and so she and I were married."

Henry was now besieged with letters from his sister, recalling with Tudor tenacity that she had always been of good mind to my Lord of Suffolk, and her brother's promise that if she married the aged and sickly monarch she would be allowed to choose her second husband herself. She took upon herself full responsibility for the marriage, knowing the executioner's axe gleamed for her husband who had broken his promise, not for her. Remembering her jewel in Henry's hat, she made over to him on her wedding day, St. Valentine's, all the plate and vessels her late husband had bestowed on her, and the choice of her special jewels. Henry's favourite jousting partner threw himself on his sovereign's mercy.

Terror seized them when they heard from Wolsey that the King had taken the news grievously and displeasantly. It was Francis who stepped into the breach by allowing her to keep her French revenue and riches, of which he could have deprived her when she married again. An Englishman of low degree suited France better as a husband for their Queen Dowager than Charles of rival Spain.

Mary, twice married within a matter of months, sailed for England with her promised dowry as a sop to her brother's anger. They were not quite sure what awaited them on the other side, but at least they were together. Mary had been spared separation and a desolate life in a foreign convent, which she felt sure would have been the death of her.

As it was, Henry received his sister and favourite with *bonhomie,* giving their marriage royal sanction by being present with the Queen in Grey Friar's Church when it was solemnized, and tournaments celebrated the event as though everything had been orderly and wonted. No one appears to have thought twice about the bridegroom's previous marital entanglements; Suffolk's procedure was to marry again and depend on a complaisant Pope to confirm the *fait accompli.*

Mary, as well as plate, jewels, gold and dowry, undertook to repay to her brother the expenses of her former marriage at the yearly rate of a thousand pounds for twenty-four years. Wolsey took the credit that the bride-

groom lost neither life nor bride, but he possibly over-
painted the King's displeasure to gain their gratitude. It
used to be said there were two obstinate men about the
King who governed everything, one Wolsey, the other
Brandon. Now the Suffolks, and he was fond of display
and cutting a figure, frequently had to retire from court
into the country to recoup when the terms fell due. That
left only Wolsey to do and undo.

Henry bounded with good spirits—Katherine was
pregnant again and as ever hope rode high. Very merry
were they that May Day when the King and his courtiers
dressed themselves as Robin Hood and his outlaws, all in
green even to their shoes. They entertained the Queen,
Mary and their ladies to a breakfast feast of venison in a
forest glade where elaborate bowers had been constructed from hawthorn, spring flowers and mosses.

When more than one were thinking that the King was
but a youngling who cared for nothing but girls and
hunting, and wasted his father's patrimony, Wolsey received a message from him. His minister was requested to
send to him a certain Act newly passed by Parliament for
his "examination and correction".

CHAPTER SIX

THE QUALITY OF MERCY

"God save our King, and bless this land
With plenty, joy and peace."

THE mayor and aldermen of London repaired to St. Paul's
on the feast of St. Matthew to return thanks to Almighty
God for the Queen, who was quick with child. Wolsey,
who never left a stone unturned, instructed them to
attend the service, and they turned out to a man.

The child was born in February and lived, but to the
disappointment of the people it was a daughter. Henry,
however, was inordinately proud of his offspring, assuring
everyone in the most besotted fashion that she never cried.
When an ambassador tactfully tempered his congratula-
tions because it was not a son, her father replied cheerfully, "We are both young; if it is a daughter this time, by
the grace of God the sons will follow."

"We are both young": we catch an echo of his mother's
voice, ten months before she died, when she comforted
his father after the death of their eldest son. Henry was
not twenty-five when he spoke these words, magnificent
with youth, lusty for life. But Katherine was six years

older, and at thirty-one she had begun to age. She had never attempted to keep up with her strenuous husband, who could tire out ten horses in the one day but not himself. In seven years of marriage she had had six pregnancies, and her figure had broadened and solidified, her serious face with its calm brow grown heavier, her copper hair begun to fade.

The child was christened Mary after her entrancing aunt. During Katherine's confinement her father King Ferdinand was finally out-tricked by death, but the news was kept from her lest it have an adverse effect. He was succeeded by his grandson Charles, the nephew Katherine had never seen.

Instead of sceptres gripped in practised old hands, young men felt them now; instead of the Henry the most youthful of the trio—France, Spain, England—he was now the senior. The newcomer Charles was the youngest at sixteen, but, self-contained as an oyster, he might have been the eldest, this new King of Spain who was never seen to smile.

Katherine, the youngest of a large family of girls, was always very much the friend of Henry's sisters. When word reached them that Margaret, Queen of Scotland, was waiting at the border for permission to enter her brother's realm, consent was at once sent, as well as everything in the way of comforts and conveniences, for Katherine knew what straits her sister-in-law was in.

She had married again, captivated by the fine figure of the youthful Earl of Angus, to the disquiet of her adopted country. The Scots reasoned that he, the "childish young" head of the powerful house of Douglas, was already great, and the Queen's marrying him made him greater still. They would not allow her to continue as regent, for that would make him too great for the peace and safety of Scotland. She had to surrender her infant son the King, since all her plans for smuggling him into England failed, and seek refuge in her brother's country.

Once over the border, in an inhospitable keep, she bore a baby daughter and nearly died. On the day her life was despaired of, her husband left both wife and daughter to return to Scotland. For that Margaret never forgave him, not so much for his defection but because he chose such a day.

At last she was well enough to travel. A nature such as hers had no half measures but swung sharply from trough to crest, crest to trough. It was thirteen years since music and bells had chimed her, a bride of fourteen, all the way into Scotland. Now her spirits rose the deeper she was carried into England and the further she left her adopted country behind. She wrote to her brother *en route* that next to God he was her only trust and confidence, and arrived by barge at Greenwich, at the palace that was so bound up with all their childhoods, to find her family waiting to welcome her with open arms.

Tournaments and pageants celebrated her homecoming, but all was not so splendid and joyous as it appeared; behind the spectacle and show could be felt the tug and strain of family ties. The first question Henry asked his sister was, "And where is my Lord Angus?" When told he had returned to Scotland, his brotherly comment came out pat, "Done like a Scot!" The jousting and festivals were on such a lavish scale, the Suffolks could not afford to keep up with them and had to retreat into the country to retrench. Margaret had never been good at lessons and time had taught her none, only served to emphasize the dominant traits of her character: her hot impatience and headstrong will that would brook no curb.

She quickly adapted herself to the procedure at her brother's court and wrote to Wolsey, excluding God in these instances, that next to the King's Grace her trust was in him. Although Henry most generously provided for her while she remained in his realm, although her clothes, furs and jewels were sent to her from Scotland, her letters to her brother and Wolsey betray her as the born borrower, each time promising this is the last, that if her request is granted she will be beholden for ever, importunate for reply yet refusing to take No, however emphatic, for answer. "I am loth to speak to the King my brother," she wrote, unabashed, to Wolsey, "because I trust you will do it for me." Religion meant little to her beyond a convenient patter; she had none of her parents' piety or Henry's liberality in almsgiving, and appalled her Scots Council by taking everything her husband left her in his will but leaving his debts unpaid.

The court sports on May Day that year were spoiled by disturbances in London so violent that the 1st May, 1517, was remembered ever afterwards as Evil May Day. Whenever there was trouble in the city, you might be sure apprentices—a rough noisy quarrelsome band ready to start a fray with or without provocation—would set it afoot.

Now the King might employ foreign craftsmen and artists to beautify his palaces, but his insular subjects detested all men not "born of the land", and trade-conscious Londoners were more envious of them than any. They muttered that foreign craftsmen took the work out of their hands and so the bread from their mouths; no one bought from them when foreign merchants were selling silks, cloths of gold, wines and other wares; foreigners brought into the country and sold cheaply the same goods that were made by honest Englishmen.

On Evil May Day, a holiday when Satan found plenty of mischief for idle hands, the apprentices' battle-cry of "Clubs! Clubs!" was heard in the streets. They marched a thousand strong to Newgate and released some of their number who were held prisoner. They attacked Spanish,

Venetian and Flemish traders, looting and destroying their homes and shops and lynching their masters. The terror lasted well into the night when they suddenly wearied and began to disband; then some three hundred were arrested and the following day another hundred were added to their ranks.

Henry swelled with disgust when he heard. Was London ruled by rascally apprentices, that strangers in their midst could not go about their lawful business without fear? What were the civic authorities doing, or not doing, to permit such things to happen? They put on mourning and hastened with gifts to Wolsey, craving his favour. Boys were hung on their masters' sign-posts before gibbets were set up.

Mothers streamed wailing to Greenwich to ask good Queen Katherine to intercede on behalf of their sons. Three queens pleaded for the prisoners, Katherine of England, Mary Dowager Queen of France, Margaret of Scotland.

Wolsey stage-managed a court scene where the prisoners were filed in, some four hundred of them. They had been in the Tower for days, crowded in narrow quarters, and each was as unkempt, dirty and tattered as his fellows. Each had a halter of rope round his neck, signifying the fate he deserved.

They blinked stupidly at the sight that met their gaze: the King himself, dazzling as the sun so that they dare not look lest they be blinded, his nobles and councillors, and the mayor and aldermen, out of their mourning and in their best robes as Wolsey had directed them to be.

Evidence was led so castigating and incriminating that each, stretching his neck in its rope collar, knew that condemnation was bound to follow. Judgement fell like the stroke of axe on block, but because they were mean fellows and not high-born, it would be the gibbet for them.

Then the man in the red coat—whom they knew to be

Cardinal Wolsey from the times they had seen him ride through the city, second only to the King himself—the man in the red coat threw himself before the throne, pleading for them. And the King bestowed his pardon.

They could scarcely believe what they saw and heard, they felt it instead. It spread like wildfire through the city. By the King's favour they were free. Tears tracked paths down black faces, bumping from their cheeks and the stubble on young chins. The high almighty King on his throne deigned to have mercy on them, the most miserable of his creatures. It was said in every shop, house and home to which an apprentice returned with the fervour of an oath, "God save the King."

London might be unsafe because of the rioting apprentices and unwholesome because of so many bodies hanging from gibbets, but nothing would deter Margaret visiting it. She wrote Wolsey she would do as he thought best and in the same sentence prayed him as heartily as she could to let her come on the morrow, trusting to God no further trouble would interfere with her plans. She had made up her restless mind to return to Scotland where she had hopes of regaining the regency, and wanted to go to Baynard's Castle before she left to collect the gear she had accumulated during her year's stay at her brother's court.

Her father had rebuilt Baynard's Castle, transforming a battlemented fortress into a pleasant palace although it had no gardens, so close to the river it appeared to spring from it. Behind it the spire of St. Paul's soared above the city and all round were churches whose bells made the air vibrant with sound.

Margaret entered England in poverty and distress. She left it in style, with jewels, plate, tapestry, arras, coin, horses—all, the English onlooker noted, at "Our King's cost".

A curious pall hovered over London like the torpor

that precedes illness. People became increasingly aware of it, found themselves waiting and listening, looking over their shoulders, as though something they did not want was about to happen. When they saw wisps of straw hanging outside certain houses, they knew what it was—the dread sweating sickness.

You might be merry at dinner and dead at supper. They said if you could stand the heat and pain of it for the first twenty-four hours, you might recover. Few did. It forced its entry into the hovels huddling in back streets and walked unbidden into manor and palace.

Henry the lion-hearted retreated before it. This was something you could not shiver with a lance or quell with a look. He and the Queen and the baby Princess moved from place to place. The pages who slept in the King's very bedchamber sickened and died; Henry stripped his household to a minimum and moved once more. He remained longest at Abingdon: there people were not continually coming to tell him about deaths as they did daily in London.

Wolsey nearly died of it, it took such toll of him that it made havoc of his appearance. His sovereign wrote to his chief minister to take every care of himself "that you may the longer endure to serve us." He could not visualize life without Wolsey who thought of everything, saw to everything, did everything. He told him the Queen his wife asked him to remember her to one she loved very well. "Both she and I will feign know when you will repair to us." That was the year Katherine had two miscarriages.

The epidemic subsided during the cold of winter, but revived the following year. Again Wolsey was struck down. His royal master concocted medicine himself to send him, christening it with a Latin name signifying Christ's Hand. He told him the good news that the Queen was pregnant.

One man in England transacted the business single-handed which occupied all the magistracies, offices and councils of Venice, civil, criminal, state and ecclesiastical. That one man was Thomas Wolsey. He distrusted parliament, never deputed, had neither party nor following, but was on a pinnacle by himself. The pinnacle was reared on his services to the King.

With gifts and benefactions, preferments and pensions, his wealth was boundless. He had grown tyrannical with power, and there were some who said his influence could not last, but it waxed, not waned. His temper became choleric and it was believed the Pope withheld the cardinal's hat a year because of his aggressiveness and ambition. He used to say, "His Majesty will do so and so." Now he said, "We shall do so and so." Very soon, as he reached the zenith of his power, he was to say, "I shall do so and so."

"Never," he was to write about this time, "was the kingdom in greater harmony and repose than now; such is the effect of my administration of justice and equity." He had sympathy with the poor and brought in decrees to help them, but he was never popular. The King was sacrosanct, and his chief minister received the redding-stroke whenever anything went wrong.

In the nine years since Henry's accession England had grown into a power to be reckoned with, due chiefly to Wolsey's skill. He was a past master at playing off the rivalry between Spain and France. The inconstant Maximilian had had an apoplectic stroke; when he died Charles would not only be King of Spain but Emperor of the Holy Roman Empire, a Caesar astride the world. Feverishly France courted England, and a treaty favourable to England, to Henry and to Wolsey was drawn up. It was handselled by the marriage alliance between the baby heir to the French throne and Henry's two-year-old daughter. The betrothal was not popular in England: the

English disliked all foreigners in general and the French in particular.

Katherine missed the banquets and entertainments that followed, as it was one of her dangerous times. A month later, in November, her child was born. The people heard the news that it was another still-birth with the greatest vexation: no heir to the throne, and their princess trysted to a Frenchman. If someone didn't look sharp, the next thing to happen would be France would marry England's princess and swallow England as her dowry.

Half a year later, in early summer, Henry fathered an illegitimate son. The mother was a girl called Elizabeth Blount, who had taken gleeful part in all the revels and romps of the young court. She had beauty, for the child was said to be goodly, like his father and mother. He was christened Henry, and his godfather was Wolsey.

Henry ordered the affair with the greatest discretion. No ambassador or envoy knew of the liaison, or got wind of the birth. He was jealous of royal prestige, and to foreigners, innured to palace excesses and scandals, his court was a model of decorum.

He was outraged when he learnt that his sister Margaret was contemplating divorcing her young husband. Katherine sent one of her ecclesiastics north to plead with her not to take such a step; Henry dispatched a stern friar to tell her from him that Satan had put such wicked ideas into her head, and what an unnatural mother she would be thus to stigmatize her infant daughter. But gentle father or vehement friar, angry brother or pained sister-in-law had not the slightest effect on Margaret.

Henry insisted upon the attendance of sufficient councillors to enable him to transact business as he moved from place to place to circumvent the epidemic, and he arranged for a relay of posts every seven hours between him and Wolsey, whom business tied to London no matter how ill he was. In the enforced absence of his chief minister, were Henry's capable hands fingering the reins of government for the first time and liking the feel of them? He drew up a memorandum of twenty-one items he wished the Lord Chancellor to put into execution. Wolsey replied what a comfort it was for him to note the King's prudence, but he must have been dismayed at this royal poaching on his preserves.

The relationship between sovereign and prelate was warm and unstrained. There was friendly competition between the King's and the Cardinal's choirs. Should a jarring note be inadvertently sounded, Wolsey was adept at transmuting the discord into harmony. There was the occasion when he showed the King and Queen over his new palace of Hampton Court, with its two hundred and eighty guest rooms and rich tapestries that were changed every week before he could tire of them. He explain how spring water, recommended by his medical advisers, was brought all the way from Coombe Hill in lead pipes.

His Majesty as he looked round saw that this sumptuous place would take five hundred servants to run if it took a man. It was a king's residence, not the home of the King's servant, and he was provoked by what he saw into demanding what his Lord Chancellor meant by building for himself so magnificent a palace.

If Wolsey was taken aback, not for a moment did he reveal it. Never at a loss for the eloquent word, he explained at some length he meant it as a gift sufficiently worthy to be offered to His Majesty. With his father's acquisitiveness, Henry was not satisfied until he held the title deeds, but Wolsey continued to address his letters from "My Manor of Hampton Court".

Henry undertook to lead a crusade against the infidel Turk in person if only God would grant him an heir. Spanish physicians came to England to see what they could do, but the child born to Katherine in November was the last she was to bear. Never again was she to know the tremulous expectancy, the leaping joy and glad fulfilment of birth.

CHAPTER SEVEN

DEFENDER OF THE FAITH

"They hae gard fill up ae punch-bowl,
   And after it they maun hae anither,
And thus the night they a' hae spent,
   Just as they had been brither and brither."

THE treaty with France provided that the two kings should meet. It was broken to the English people that the meeting was to take place in France by stressing that although their king was crossing the water he was convening with his French counterpart on English soil.

Wherever Henry was he always filled the picture, not only because he was king but because he was Henry. Routine could not harness his flamboyant personality, so that even a practice hour at the butts or in the tilt-yard became a gala occasion for those who accompanied him. Now as he passed through the countryside on his way to the coast, every moment of his passage to those who watched him go by was a picked one. The approbation of the populace was so well justified by his person that his affability towards them surrounded him like a halo.

Never had they seen anything like this before: the

procession winding through the vernal May landscape seemed endless. This would give these Frenchies something to stare at. And at the heart of the surge and sway and swirl of movement was the King himself, so eye-filling that after he had passed there was no sense of flatness, only pride that they had beheld one so worth the seeing. When they thought of him afterwards, he proceeded through their minds like a pageant, and when they saw a goldfinch, with its swelling coloured breast and wings barred with gold, they would wag their heads at it, addressing it as King Hal.

At Canterbury the King and Queen paused to keep holy Pentecost. It was there Henry heard that Spanish ships bringing Charles to England had been sighted off Dover. Charles was now King and Emperor. The man who ruled over one of the greatest accumulations of territories in history considered Henry important enough to visit, crossing continent and channel to do so, scrambling to get in before his meeting with the rival Francis. Well might Wolsey congratulate himself on the position England had attained. France and the Empire—whichever had not England as its ally was perilously outbalanced.

Wolsey put out in a small boat to meet their visitor, and conducted him to Dover Castle, where the Emperor, tired out after a stormy voyage, retired to bed. In the middle of the night he was disturbed by the stir of arrival—the King of England had ridden from Canterbury by torchlight to greet him. Emperor and King met at the top of the stairs, and nephew was embraced by his bounding uncle-in-law. Together they sat up half the night talking in the keep stateroom.

So this was Charles, King of Spain and its South American colonies, of the Kingdoms of Sicily and Naples, Emperor of Austria and the Low Countries, which included the Netherlands, England's best foreign customer. He was not tall, neither was he small; his pale face, white after his sea journey, was made ugly by the protruding Hapsburg underlip, animated only by bright and intelligent eyes. His gravity was such that he might have been a grandfather instead of twenty, and he had as much charm as a lamp without a wick has light. Nothing here to pique Henry or challenge his competitive instincts. It was state business they talked as night winds drummed on old walls and whistled down the chimney.

It was state business they talked next day as they rode side by side to Canterbury, bridles ringing and jingling. Katherine met her unknown nephew joyfully, and for the first time Mary Tudor and the man to whom she had been betrothed came face to face. Every English pair of eyes was upon him, watching what he felt as he looked at the loveliest woman in the country. He appeared dejected, and refused to dance.

A few days later Charles took ship for Flanders, and Henry sailed in *The Great Harry* for France, but before parting they agreed to meet again at Calais after Henry's rendezvous with Francis. What they had been conferring must be bound and riveted by treaty.

Henry's former advent in France was like a dress rehearsal compared to this. In his retinue marched over four and a half thousand persons, including dukes, earls, marquises, bishops, barons, knights. The Queen was accompanied by a train of nearly thirteen hundred. Everything Wolsey's resourceful brain could invent materialized to impress the French with the wealth and power of England. A palace of art was one building to be erected which, although temporary, was so exquisite Italians declared it might have been designed by Leonardo da Vinci himself.

The ground where the kings were to meet lay between two castles still manned by English soldiers, so could be called English soil. So lavish was the display, the site became known as the Field of Cloth of Gold. In the vast courtyard of the English pavilion a fountain sprayed red, white and claret wine. Inside, the Tudor rose bloomed everywhere, flowering on hangings and curtains, entwining silver drinking vessels and plates, blossoming on the curious foreign glass in the windows. The French pavilion had to outmatch it if possible, no matter what it cost. Its motif was a midnight-blue ceiling of rich stuffs in which sparkled and glittered solid gold stars.

The King of England started from English-held Guisnes at the same time as the King of France started from Ardes, to meet in the valley between the two towns. As French and English converged, suspicion of French designs broke over the English ranks, but it was overcome.

Alone the two kings rode out to meet each other. A breathless silence hung over the waiting, watching multitudes, and a slight, almost imperceptible stir, like an escaped sigh, passed over both retinues. The sovereigns embraced on horseback, and then again on foot.

Everything here to rival and compete with the King of England. Francis was as tall, might even be taller (or perhaps it was only his long lean legs that gave that impression), as strong and as magnificently garbed, and he carried himself valorously, like a prince.

"I never saw Prince with my eyes that might of my heart be more loved," Henry told him. "And for your love I have crossed the seas, into the furthest frontier of my realm, to see you, which doing now gladdens me." Francis was as forthcoming in return, with a playful allusion to Henry as "my prisoner".

The French had to admit that King Henry was a very handsome prince. They liked his manner, which struck them as gentle and gracious, and his becoming red beard. They noted their monarch was taller, but the English one undoubtedly had the better-looking face. Indeed beside his French counterpart, his fair skin made him appear to them almost womanly. It was like seraph meeting Lucifer.

For sixteen gilded days the two retinues remained together, entertaining each other, exchanging compliments. The two kings held the field against all comers, no one could say which outshone the other. They breakfasted together, gave gifts to one another, professed eternal amity, for all the world to see the fastest friends in Christendom. "These sovereigns," commented a penetrating Venetian, "hate each other very cordially."

There was no insincerity between the two queens; both devout and virtuous women, they were kindred spirits. Katherine considered no time so much wasted as that passed in dressing and adorning herself. Even if Queen Claude had not been pregnant, her nature was as retiring, and it was Mary, Dowager Queen of France, who rode between her brother and the King of France.

Only French memoirs record the incident when their king threw the English one. It was an unrehearsed occasion: Henry, hearty after beating Francis at archery, suddenly seized the tall Frenchman by the collar, saying, "Come, you shall wrestle with me." Francis was taken off his guard, but recovered quickly. The struggle that followed was over almost before it had begun. To the horror of the two queens and the watching courtiers they saw and heard the resounding thud as England's king was thrown to the ground.

Never had such a thing happened to him in his life before. Henry rose, his big face reddening until it flared scarlet. "Again!" he said in a voice of thunder. But the two queens fussed forward, courtiers flocked round. Everyone talked animatedly about nothing in particular, no one looked at anyone else, and the crisis passed by pretending it had not taken place.

The man responsible for the Field of Cloth of Gold had outgrown his humble cassock and uncaparisoned steed.

Cardinal Wolsey was clad in crimson satin from head to foot, his mule's trappings were of gold, he was accompanied by two hundred gentlemen, and he had a bodyguard of two hunderd archers. Francis, King of France, received him as his equal; when he celebrated mass on the last day bishops invested him with his robes and put sandals on his feet, and water to wash his hands was brought to him by some of the chief English nobles.

In air over-sweet with incense and flowers, with enormous golden candlesticks blazing like suns, with altars hung with cloth of gold tissue and golden images of the twelve Apostles looking blankly on, Thomas Wolsey reached the height of his splendour. This was what he had brought about, the meeting of two nations, hereditary enemies, in concord and love. Yet there was as little permanence in this peace as there was in the showy chapel, built in one night, in which he sang mass. Wolsey knew that in the war that was bound to break between France and Spain, England had already elected to side with Spain.

After the painted spectacle and parade of chivalry, transactions and acts. Henry, on his way back to England, met Charles at the Flemish town of Gravelines, and together they repaired to Calais. The Emperor was unlucky with weather; a great wind blew the roof of the conference hall away, but negotiations were satisfactorily completed. Henry bound himself to proceed no further in the marriage between Princess Mary and the Dauphin, and Charles bound himself to proceed no further in that between himself and Francis's little daughter. Not included but implicit in the treaty was the proviso that Charles should marry Henry's daughter himself. Wolsey's perquisite was the Emperor's promise to help him gain St. Peter's chair when it should fall vacant.

Once home, Henry for the remaining six months of the year spent his time hunting: from daybreak to sundown he was in the saddle. "He spares no pains to convert the sport of hunting into a martyrdom," remarked a sedentary bishop. Such exercise was excessive even for him, as though by thrashing his body tired he hoped to wear down a problem that threatened.

Katherine was not going to have another child. She was thirty-five now, and for two years there had been no quickening. Francis had said, "My brother of England has no son because, although a young and handsome man, he keeps an old and ugly wife." But Katherine had not always been old. The harvest of eight pregnancies was one small daughter, pale as an ear of wheat, and no heir. The humblest peasant in his realm took it as reproach if he had no male issue, and he, Henry King of England, had no heir to succeed him. Yet his illegitimate son was growing in beauty and in strength. Only one Being was strong enough, powerful enough, omnipotent enough to lay this rod upon a sovereign He had favoured in every other way, and that one Being was God. The rod pointed at Henry's marriage to his brother's widow. Katherine's little waxen babies must be the token of His displeasure at their union.

Henry's loyal championship of the Pope did the religion in which he was cradled every credit. It did not matter whether he were the belligerent Julius or the peaceful Leo, Henry chivalrously defended him because he was the custodian of the Church, and in proof of this had taken up arms. His religion had a strong theological bent; he enjoyed discussing and amicably disputing with scholars and prelates. So incited was he on reading a heretical book by a pestilent German called Martin Luther that he wrote to Pope Leo he must defend the Church with his pen as well as his sword.

He took two years to write his book, dedicating to the Pope the first offerings of his intellect and his little erudition. The brilliant Wolsey was too wise to criticize or edit it, the author too shrewd to think it worthy of the

Cardinal's high-flown praise; nevertheless he was proud of his brain child. It never, however, takes wings like his music and songs; instead it remains earth-bound, bogged down by long-winded rhetoric.

Of marriage Henry wrote sententiously: "The insipid water of concupiscence is turned by the hidden grace of God into the finest flavour. Whom God hath joined together let no man put asunder." Had God joined him and Katherine together? Not if the words in Leviticus were remembered: "And if a man shall take his brother's wife, it is an unclean thing . . . they shall be childless." He and Katherine were not childless, there was Mary of whom Henry was very fond, but they were sonless. It was of course impossible for Henry to do wrong, but he might in innocence have committed an illegal act by taking Arthur's widow. There was no such thing as an illegal marriage: a marriage that was not legal was not marriage. Supposing he and Katherine were not married at all, but had quite inadvertently—to neither could blame be imputed—been living in mortal sin all along? To neither could blame be imputed so long as they had been living together believing they were married. It was a different matter when doubts arose and conscience quirked.

A copy of Henry's book bound in cloth of gold was presented to Leo, patron of literature, who admired the binding and trim decking. He read five pages there and then, exclaiming at every second line. His Holiness remarked he was surprised at such a book coming from the King's grace, so necessarily occupied in other feats—men who had spent all their lives in study could not bring forth the like of this. He promulgated a bull which conferred on England's sovereign the superb title Defender of the Faith.

This distinction meant much to the diligent author, and the bull was received with great ceremonial. The new name rang the length of the hall as the heralds proclaimed it again and again. Patch, the King's fool, wanted to know why his master was so jocund. "Because of my new title," answered the King. "Prithee, good Harry," pattered the jester, "let thee and I defend one another and leave the Faith alone to defend itself."

The very diversity of Charles's far-flung empire made it difficult, if not impossible, to rule, for when there was peace in one quarter, there was trouble brewing and uprising elsewhere. It was in his realms too that men were beginning to dispute the indisputable, the Holy Roman Catholic Church, and heresy called for instantaneous suppression before it could run riot.

France, feeling herself encircled by her rival's spreading domains, took advantage of every opportunity that offered when Charles was hard pressed. The gnawing friction between them broke, as everyone knew was inevitable sooner or later, into open warfare, and each called on Henry to fulfil his treaty obligation by coming to his assistance.

For a stopgap measure Wolsey was dispatched to France to attempt to negotiate a truce between the two powers. Henry was not ready for war. His father's treasure was exhausted; money and an army would have to be raised. Time was essential, and it was time Wolsey played for on his mission, diplomatically falling ill when necessary. Henry could only maintain his balance between Charles and Francis so long as neither had the mastery; the longer, therefore, they were kept apart the better it suited him. When the breach came, he had no intention of standing aloof and letting the contenders fight it out to the death between them. It would be Charles's side, not Francis's, on which Henry would throw England's weight.

That had been arranged between king and minister before the Cardinal crossed the Channel, and it was not a noble part for them to play. While Wolsey swore friendship to Francis, he was stroking the t's and dotting the i's of the treaty with Charles. The French with their logical minds could not credit the English were playing them false: surely England's policy would be to build up her strength and consolidate her reserves while the two rivals weakened themselves with war, leaving her in an unassailable position.

Henry's motive for aligning himself actively with Charles when he could have been neutral was that he was certain Charles would win, and he wanted to share in not only the defeat of Francis but the spoils. His minister's policy had been pro-French in the past. There are two schools of thought why Wolsey, the patriotic, skilled diplomatist, chose war rather than peace, to intrigue instead of to mediate. Either he took a gambler's risk, displaying before Henry the chance of recovering his rights to the crown of France to divert his attention from home affairs which were heading for ruin, or, and this is the more likely, he put himself first, and hitched England to Charles's star, because Charles, ruler of the Holy Catholic Empire, had promised him St. Peter's throne when it fell vacant.

While Wolsey was absent, Henry again handled state affairs. He was not like the Cardinal, who did everything himself and could not depute. Henry delegated, but he kept up his sleeve the master stroke of the last word. When his chief minister returned, King and Cardinal worked smoothly enough together in that Wolsey did the work and Henry retained the power of veto.

Three months after he had handled Henry's book, Pope Leo died. At once kings, princes, prelates, sprang into action to have the Holy See filled by their nominee. The lobbying, the pulling of wires, the jockeying for position, the heavy pressure brought to bear were intense as France tried for the election of a French delegate and the Empire an imperial one. In Rome the cardinals met to choose Leo's successor in an atmosphere that resembled a cockpit rather than conclave. Of them Charles's envoy wrote, "There cannot be so much hatred and so many devils in hell as among these cardinals."

Wolsey never had the ghost of a chance: for close on four centuries no Englishman had attained the Papacy, which had see-sawed between Spain and France. When his nominator arrived in Rome he learnt that Charles, not Francis, had won the papal stakes. The new Vicar of Christ was a Netherlander who had been Charles's tutor: such was the decayed condition of the Papacy, his honesty made him one of the most unpopular pontiffs ever to be enthroned.

As the days of the new year lengthened into spring, Wolsey busied himself preparing for war with as many delaying tactics as he could devise, for England was anything but ready. The lines running from nose to mouth on his strong, once handsome face were becoming more deeply etched. His temper was growing shorter, and there were occasions when he would let fly a volley of abuse should he be crossed. In an excess of fury, he even laid hands on an unfortunate nuncio who he believed was sending unfavourable reports of him to France.

By this time Henry had had two known mistresses, the fair-haired Elizabeth Blount and the current dark-haired Mistress Carey. His morals were not unduly lax according to the standards of his day, and he was no libertine like Francis.

Mistress Carey was one of Katherine's maids-in-waiting and until lately, when she married, had been Mary Boleyn. Her father, Sir Thomas Boleyn, had spent his time during the past few years posting as envoy between France and England, but now war was imminent he brought his younger daughter Anne home with him. Like her sister Mary, she had been educated in France, one of three hundred girls in Queen Claude's household, where she was taught to sing, dance, work and pray.

She dances across the page for the first time at a court revel, very young, light of heart, with more than one string to her bow. Her blue-black hair and mirthful dark eyes betrayed her Irish ancestry. She did not wear her very long hair smoothly coifed like the English girls, but floating free after the French fashion, interlaced with jewels since this was a special occasion. She was slight, and as alive as a bird propelled by its own song, with a slender neck and the flexible throat of the singer. She inspired the poet Wyatt to write sonnets, and although he was married he paid advances to her, but it was Henry Percy she favoured. So much in love were they, they plighted their troth, the Earl's son and the merchant's granddaughter.

Mary was the King's mistress, and their father began to receive honour after honour: every year a new benefaction filled the Boleyn cornucopia. But Mary remained Mistress Carey. Henry kept the liaison very much in the background. He conceded not an iota of the deference due to the Queen as his consort and wife, but Katherine's face began to wear the sorrowful look of one who accepts that her prayers will go unanswered.

CHAPTER EIGHTH

DIPLOMATIC REVERSAL

"The eagle's force subdues each bird that flies:
   What metal can resist the flaming fire?
Doth not the sun dazzle the fairest eyes,
   And melt the ice, and make the frost retire?
The hardest stones are pierced through with tools,
The wisest are with princes made but fools."
                                    —*Henry VIII*

HENRY played host to Charles again; this time the Emperor stayed some weeks instead of several days. He arrived with a large retinue of Spanish grandees and German nobles, and instead of flying spray salting their deliberations, Henry seized the opportunity to entertain his visitor in fitting manner. London fairly crackled with bonfires and flamed with torches; pageants and processions made lively the summer streets. A contemporary packed the six weeks of fête into a nutshell with the words, "Nothing lacked that could be gotten to cheer the Emperor and his lords, and all that came in his company were highly feasted." But Charles gives the impression of not being a very disportive guest, the one serious note in the fanfare.

Soon after his arrival Henry took him to Greenwich, to that favourite palace where the river wound. They landed by barge, climbing the water stairs. Waiting for them, framed in the principal doorway, stood Queen Katherine, holding by the hand Charles's future bride, the Princess Mary.

She was six years old, a tiny thing with brown eyes and hair the Tudor fairness. Already she could talk to foreigners in their own tongue and play the harpsichord with nimbleness. Henry thought the world of her. He was fond of children, and this clever little girl was his own daughter, not someone else's. Children for their part felt at home with his uninhibited personality. To Mary her father was the world; in his presence everything that was big, warm and splendid happened all at the one time.

She saw something of her future bridegroom during his stay, and the grave young man and small child drew together in a kind of mannered courtship. Already she was treated as Empress, and it was thus she, young as she was, deported herself. Charles signed the matrimonial treaty while he was in England, binding himself to marry her when she reached the age of twelve.

The agreement provided that if Henry had no son to succeed him, the eldest male child born to Charles and Mary should become King of England. It was a very full moment for Henry: his daughter to marry not a king's son but the Emperor himself, his grandson maybe not only to rule England but the Empire.

Charles was anxious for his bride to be sent to Spain where she could be educated as his wife, but every time the point was raised in the years to come Henry adroitly turned it aside. The Princess was too young as yet to stand a sea journey, or be moved from her native air, and where in all of Christendom could the Emperor find a more fit mistress to bring up his future wife after the manner of Spain than her own mother?

She was, however, subjected to a rigid education which excluded all idle books of chivalry and romance; the few stories allowed for her recreation were historical, sacred or classical. She had to concentrate on the Gospels night and morning, selected portions of the Old Testament, the Holy Fathers, and Latin and Greek masters. The "right merry and joyous" infant with her father's rosy cheeks grew into a pallid, spare, short-sighted scholar before she was twelve.

Henry, now irrevocably welded to Charles, declared war on Francis. It was pleasant to believe that the over-taxed French wanted to change their king and were crying, *"Vive le roi d'Angleterre!"* But nothing was more costly than war, and for the first time in his life Henry lacked money. Wolsey, who saw to everything, had to apply himself to the vital task of filling the emptied coffers. He as chief minister was responsible for the pro-Emperor policy, on which he and Henry had staked their all.

The rest of the country lacked their enthusiasm. War with France always meant war on two fronts: the moment an English army left its island base, the Scots would be across the border in their hordes to aid their French allies.

Wolsey began by instituting "voluntary" loans; his names for his various measures all turned out painful misnomers. The country responded handsomely enough, London alone supplying £20,000 with admirable promptitude, but the sums brought in, although large, were trifling to mount a full-scale invasion, and were swallowed up by some abortive naval engagements, the only attacks made that year. There was nothing else for it, or Wolsey would have done it: Parliament would have to be summoned and made to supply money for the war.

Parliament heard him in what the Cardinal himself described as a marvellous obstinate silence. Not a word could he extort from them, no matter how he railed and how shrilly he demanded some reasonable answer. Very humbly the Speaker intimated that the Members were refusing to speak except through him, their common mouth, and they would not give voice in the Cardinal's presence. Discomfited, Wolsey had to retire.

A delegation asked him to prevail upon the King to accept half of the enormous sum claimed. Wolsey spoke no more than the truth when he told them he would rather have his tongue plucked out of his head with red-hot pincers than induce the King to do any such thing. It took Parliament a hundred days before they granted appreciably less than two-thirds of the required sum.

As with all autocrats, the first step of his climb-down altered irretrievably Wolsey's direction. From that moment it was descent, not ascent. This was the first time he had failed the King, as he was to fail in his other attempts to raise money for an unpopular war. His position, alone on his pinnacle, was only tenable so long as the foundation on which it was reared did not move, and Wolsey's foundation was his master the King. The slightest shift in the substructure and fissure zigzagged from base to apex.

Nothing was going right for Henry. Gone were these halcyon days when life showered on him everything he could desire without the asking—save a son. He heard himself praised in Parliament as an ideal king of great judgement, learning, experience and diligence, yet its members only voted with the greatest reluctance part of the sum demanded. (Their sovereign noted that Parliament could not be browbeaten as Wolsey had attempted to do: Parliament should be handled as a means, not an end. The goose would not lay its golden eggs if it were badgered from its nest.) His subjects were complaining they shouldn't be asked to burn their fingers taking chestnuts out of the fire for the Emperor. Could they or would they not see that through war with France their all-wise king would recover his right to the French crown? Francis would receive from Henry's hand what King Richard had received from Henry's father on Bosworth Moor—defeat and death.

The largest army to leave England for a hundred years sailed for Calais before the end of August, delayed until autumn by the emptiness of the exchequer and the usual administrative hold-ups. It advanced to within forty miles of Paris, capturing all towns on the way, when it had to fall back on Calais as the Emperor's joint invasion did not materialize and winter was setting in. Only the dread of a second Flodden kept the Scots from pouring over the defenceless border.

Nothing was going right for Wolsey. The Pope died, his only popular act since he became pontiff less than two short years ago, and the citizens of Rome in their gratitude for his death erected a statue to his doctor. Wolsey told Henry he would rather continue in his service than be ten Popes, nevertheless he raised heaven and earth to be elected. Charles obligingly wrote a letter in his favour, but did not send it until after the election, when his own nominee was chosen.

The following year Charles made up for his inactivity and invaded France, laying siege to Marseilles. No attempt was made to help him from the English side. Henry had neither the heart nor the resources, and Wolsey was playing tit for tat with the Emperor. In the unpleasant hiatus between Henry's and Charles's invasions, the Cardinal had time to wonder if by aiding and abetting the Emperor England was not nourishing an ally who could overrun the world. Uneasily he watched the new Pope, in an effort to redress the imperial predominance, throw his weight on the opposite side. No longer was England the crucial balance between two forces: to keep any position at all she had to hop from side to side. Very tentative overtures were made to Francis.

It looked as though what was tentative would shortly be consolidated; the French defended Marseilles with spirited stubbornness. It did not fall and the imperial army were forced to retreat towards Italy before the onslaught of winter.

All would have been well for Francis had he been content to defend his kingdom, but success went to his over-ambitious head. He had had victories and conquests in the past when he had taken the offensive; this time he would regain the glittering prize of Milan. He crossed the Alps with his army. As he sat down to besiege Pavia, astrologers foretold from the sky what any general knew, that his star was on the wane.

The English King was in bed when an excited courier arrived to tell him the startling news that imperial troops had annihilated the French army and taken their sovereign prisoner. Henry's joy knew no bounds. "You are as welcome as the Angel Gabriel was to the Virgin Mary," he declared lyrically to the messenger, and leapt out of bed to break the good news to Katherine himself.

The Queen began to smile again: she dreaded when English policy veered towards Francis, away from the nephew she longed to see her son-in-law. Henry ordered London to celebrate the capture of the French King, bonfires were lit and free wine dispensed to the citizens The city rang with the music of minstrels and the songs of children, and the King and Queen attended a jubilant *Te Deum* in St. Paul's with the foreign ambassadors. To Henry the crown of France was near as touching.

The historic victory was won on the Emperor's birthday. Charles received the news of the complete defeat of the French and the capture of Francis with none of Henry's triumphant exuberance, but with a self-restraint that awed the world into admiration. At twenty-five years of age he was a Caesar astride the globe, in a position to dictate to Christian and infidel alike.

Henry, riding the crest of his ally's conquest, dispatched envoys to Spain proposing the Emperor should depose Francis and invade France with England to satisfy their just claims. Unhappily Wolsey had to fall in with his master's plans, which would inflate the Emperor's already dangerous influence to terrifying proportions.

An invasion of France meant money would have to be raised, and quickly. Wolsey dare not summon Parliament again so he proposed what he called an Amicable Grant, trying to soften the tax by explaining it was necessary for the King to invade France in person and he must go as a prince, which meant lavish supplies. But the old magic no longer worked. The Amicable Grant failed, as did the Benevolent one hastily instituted to take its place.

A nameless London councillor shot out at the great Cardinal that benevolences were illegal, giving chapter and verse for the statute. The men of Kent, who were always troublesome because they would not truckle, said darkly there would be no rest from such payments as long as *some one* was living, and openly refused to pay. So did East Anglia; the agitation in Norfolk and Suffolk reached violence. It was not only Wolsey who was blamed; no longer could the King do no wrong. He was compared most unfavourably to his father by the lieges. They pointed out to a startled Archbishop that King Henry had not one foot of land more in France than had his noble father, who lacked neither riches nor wisdom to win the kingdom of France if he had thought it expedient.

The situation was saved by Henry's denying any knowledge of Wolsey's demand for a sixth of every man's substance. He only wished to receive, he said, such money as his subjects would freely give him. As his subjects were obviously not in a mood to grant him a groat, the fatal taxes were dropped, a royal pardon issued to all who had been arrested for refusing to pay, and the country told their sovereign had given up all thoughts of his expedition to France. The people muttered amongst themselves that Wolsey for private gain and ambition had talked an unwilling king into going to war.

Rumour was darting and flickering like a snake's tongue, so scintillant it left no trace and one wondered if it had been, that Charles was going to repudiate his obligation to marry Henry's daughter. It forked to Princess Mary's ears, who wore Spanish dress to accustom herself to it. It was noticed she whitened when she heard her bridegroom was thinking of taking another cousin for his wife.

A beset Wolsey wrote an elaborate letter to the Emperor, enclosing an emerald ring from his small bride-elect, telling him it would prove how faithful she was to him, as she prayed he would keep constant to her. The Emperor stuck Mary's ring on his little finger as far as it would go, and said to the English ambassadors he would wear it for her sake.

They came no further speed with him. He had not defeated Francis to exalt his uncle-in-law, and showed no disposition to share a victory he had won alone with an ally who had stood idly by.

Home truths from the imperial side made the meeting uncomfortable. The Emperor knew all about the overtures to France, that Wolsey had called him a faithless liar and insulted his ambassador. When he was asked by the envoys for the return of the five hundred thousand crowns their king claimed he had borrowed, they were told the Emperor was short of money too. The Englishmen saw it was needless to blow any longer at a dead coal, but reeled when they heard if they wanted him to marry their lady princess she must be brought to Spain at once with her dowry of £80,000.

Henry's pro-Emperor policy rattled in ruins about

him; the dreams of his grandson succeeding to the English and Imperial throne dissolved into thin air, and the crown of France for himself proved delusion. Coldly he acquiesced when Charles asked to be freed from his engagement to Mary that he could marry Isabella of Portugal—first his sister, then his daughter. He made what capital he could out of his formal assent by demanding repayment of what his nephew owed him, but he did not recover a penny.

By the time Francis had bought his freedom at the price of promises he had no intention of keeping, England had negotiated a treaty of amity with France. Instead of an Emperor who held the corners of the earth in his hands, Henry had for his allies the Pope, a pontiff who trembled with irresolution, and a Lucifer who had fallen from heaven, cut down to the ground.

No longer was Mary, his daughter, called Empress. Her dark-eyed suitor was going to marry not a little girl of nine but a grown-up princess who was not only beautiful but had a dowry of one million crowns. Mary's small face tightened and her mouth compressed, bearing the unbearable.

The French Queen Claude had died, and there was talk of her marriage to the King of France: that was what her father desired above all else to revenge himself on the Emperor. To be Queen was not the same as Empress, the French King not the same as the darkling Spaniard, but it was second best and second best was better than nothing, particularly when her father had set his heart on it. Oh, if only she were more than nine, and such a small puny nine at that. What was the good of making herself old and wise with lessons when she looked so much younger than she even was?

She was sent to Ludlow Castle, on the marches of Wales, with a court of her own and state as befitted the King's daughter. In the same year her father's natural son, the child he had by Elizabeth Blount—terrible to think he was Mary's half brother—was created Duke of Richmond and Somerset and treated as heir apparent. It was said the six-year-old boy was to take precedence over all the nobility and over Princess Mary herself. All the church ceremonial that accompanied the investiture would not bless such a proceeding, not if they sprinkled the whole of the river Jordan on it. Her mother seemed very far away. If the King of France failed, Mary was to be affianced to his son, but what was a boy groom compared to the one she had lost, so nobly older than she?

No longer was Henry's favour curried and courted from every quarter of the globe; England was nothing compared to what she had been twelve years ago. That year it rained from November until the end of January: it was as though the land were accursed. The succession—the succession—the succession: persistent as the rain from leaden skies, thoughts of the succession dripped through Henry's mind.

If he died without a successor there would be anarchy, and he was not going to die without an heir, to toss the Tudor crown to be fought for by men who had no more claim to it than their common greed. Norfolk was one. Norfolk had to be ridden on a tighter rein than ever, now the son had succeeded the father; and there were plenty of others avid to stake their claim if Henry let them. But he was a man in his prime, as strong and able to have sons as he was to rule.

There was of course Mary. The people thought a woman could not come to the throne; Henry of course knew there was no law against it. But Mary did not secure the succession. She was delicate for one thing, always ailing, and might not reach maturity. If she did and married a subject, exactly the same conflicts would arise that had created the Wars of the Roses. If she married a foreign prince, her subjects would be jealous of foreign influence and the fear of foreign dominance would breed rebellion.

He had considered entailing the succession on his illegitimate son, which was why the boy had been created Duke of Richmond and Somerset and heaped with family titles. But the rights of a natural son to the throne could be disputed after the father was dead, so Henry's illegitimate child no more secured the succession than his legitimate daughter.

At last his sister Margaret, the Queen of Scotland, achieved what for eight years she had been working for, a divorce, and married for the third time. Henry boiled over with righteous anger that his sister, instead of behaving like a noble princess, could do anything so unnatural. When he learnt the annulment had been confirmed by the Pope, he wrote scathingly to her of the shameless sentence sent from Rome which plainly revealed how unlawfully it had been handled.

If the Pope could supply on the flimsiest pretexts possible an annulment for Margaret, who was a shame and disgrace to all her family, why should he not provide one for Henry, Defender of the Faith and ornament of rectitude, on lawful grounds? Never would Henry, unlike Margaret, stoop to do anything that was illegal or unorthodox. Every step he took must be sanctified by the Church and confirmed by law.

CHAPTER NINE

LADY-IN-WAITING

"Our King he has a secret to tell,
And ay well keepit it must be."

A SERIOUS drought followed the rains, which returned in April and continued for eight weeks. Grain rotted in the soaking soil, and there was no hay or straw for fodder. Animals died, and a plague attacked the remaining cattle. Their eyes sank back into their heads and their thin sides shuddered as they coughed themselves to death. The Hand of God lay heavily on the land, but the people did not place the blame at heaven's door. Soured with taxes at home and sullen with failure abroad, they held the Cardinal responsible for all their ills, while the King's name no longer roused them to patriotic ardour.

The first steps towards the annulment of his marriage to Katherine were taken before Anne Boleyn caught Henry's fancy. She had been dismissed from court and sent back to her father's house by Wolsey when he discovered she and Lord Percy had entered into a love troth. That was something for which Anne never forgave the Cardinal: she held him and him alone answerable when their contract was dissolved and her young lover married to the lord steward's daughter.

The Anne Boleyn who returned to court was not quite the same as the Anne Boleyn who had left it. Locked away for all time was the tremulous ecstasy of first love, and what took its place was neither tremulous nor ecstatic. Diamond bright, she scintillated where once she had sparkled. It is not known when the King's small eyes marked her out as his; probably it was her gaiety that attracted him. She had none of her mistress Queen Katherine's learning, but everything she did was characteristic and she was feminine to the core. She had no great beauty but she had the wit and charm to transform defects into attractions. She hid a strawberry mark on her neck with an ornamental collar band which her fellow maids of honour thought so beguiling they all began to wear collar bands. They copied too the long hanging sleeves she had brought from France, although they were not hiding as she was a tiny malformation on her left hand. She was very graceful dancing the leaping English dances, and when she sang, the oldest turned his head to listen.

If Henry ever thought to substitute Anne for his mistress, Mary Carey, he soon discovered that Anne was not so comfortable as her sister. It has been said that her uncle, the Duke of Norfolk, primed her to set her sights for the highest dignity of all and not to become the King's mistress, but no amount of priming could have tutored a lady-in-waiting at Henry's court to hold His Majesty at arm's length.

Anne handled the situation to the manner born. She had the example of her own sister before her. To be the King's mistress had not advanced Mary in any way, while his earlier love, Elizabeth Blount, who had borne him a son, had been married off to an obscure knight. By the time she knew he was in love with her, all the cards were in Anne's hands, although it is unlikely they were the

95

cards she would have chosen. "Wild for to hold, though I seem tame," she is described in a sonnet of Wyatt's. Henry became beglamoured of her before he knew where he was and he could not break from her spell. "My great folly" he describes it in one of his letters to her: his passion for her was his only folly in a life he mastered as he did a horse. The situation did not last for a year or two, but for at least six years before actual marriage. That it trailed on too long was Anne's tragedy; when marriage did come, Henry's passion was over-spent.

Katherine's unhappiness played on her health; she was like an instrument whose strings are broken or frayed. Her husband never came to her apartments now and there was no longer the communion between them of unspoken question and answer when they were apart. They had shared so much in the past that neither could say which was the giver and who the taker, only that they belonged to one another. No longer warmed by the sun of his presence, her life was emptied; and the occasions when she was at his side as his consort only served to heighten her loneliness without him.

No longer did she advise or was kept advised on state affairs, Spain was the enemy now, France the ally. She would have died content to think of Mary safe in her native land as Empress, but that would never be—her nephew had married Isabella of Portugal. She had not even her beloved little daughter beside her—Mary had been sent to luckless Ludlow Castle where Katherine had journeyed with her boy-husband after their marriage a lifetime ago, and where he had died. Mary had been provided with a more honourable court than had even Arthur, Prince of Wales. Her father wanted the King of France to marry her, so she must have the state befitting his daughter and the future French queen. Again the face of Francis I rose before Katherine as she had seen it at the Field of Cloth of Gold, beginning to lose its perfect oval, the strong nose beginning to thicken, the dissipated eyes under the drooped lids, the full lips smiling redly above the black beard.

It was Wolsey who had to be thanked for the rupture with Charles and strengthening friendship with France. Now Henry was not in the Spanish camp, he naturally felt safer on Francis's side: after all, France boasted four times the inhabitants that England had. But Wolsey—for long enough Katherine's communications with the Cardinal had been more and more distant. There were stirrings behind the scenes. She only heard faint whispers but enough to tell her something was afoot, something inimical to her.

A French bishop, over with a delegation to consider the alliance between the English princess and his king, questioned Henry about his marriage to Katherine of Aragon. If it were not valid (how could it be argued a marriage was not valid after eighteen years?), then his daughter Mary he wished to marry to their sovereign could not be legitimate. As though Henry's mind were not fecund enough with probings and findings without this further fertilization.

What was he discussing with all these doctors and divines, theologians and jurists who were stealthily finding their way to him? She heard of his very secret visit to Wolsey's house—Wolsey was at the foot of everything; the Archbishop of Canterbury was present. He was to whisper in Katherine's ear four Latin words which signified the wrath of a king meant death.

Footsteps on unknown errands, padding into silence, hurrying to the King with news, all were gathered into Henry's when he visited her in her apartments. He was a big man and they seemed to shake the foundations. When was the last time he had been here, and why had he come?

Did she really want to know when she heard him tell

her that for the past eighteen years they had been cohabiting, unmarried? Katherine was Arthur's widow, not Henry's wife. That was why God had punished them by the deaths of all their male children. Katherine must now choose a place where she could retire, for Henry's conscience, reinforced with Holy Writ, would not permit him to continue living in mortal sin.

Henry took it for granted he could read Katherine like a book: a dutiful, devoted and faithful helpmeet who had always put him first and deferred to his slightest wish would accept the inevitable with a brave submissiveness. Above all she would be reasonable.

What happened was so unforeseen he found himself totally unprepared to cope with it. Katherine burst into tears. She lifted up her face and wept without restraint, as women have wept since Biblical times, when they were taken captive, mourning for their dead, forsaken in some alien land.

Anything he could have borne, so well accoutred he would have welcomed debate, but not this. For this he had neither weapon nor balm. Covered with confusion, he beat a hasty retreat. "All shall be done for the best," he told her hurriedly before he left, and found himself begging her not to divulge what he had told her.

He was under the quite mistaken impression that what was termed "the King's great matter" was known to no one but the prelates with whom he had discussed it. As a matter of fact all London knew of it. It was the burning topic discussed behind the painted lattices of inns, in the taverns in East Cheap, in the Grass, Fish and Meat Markets, by the sober merchants as they went in and out of their halls. It might have been proclaimed by the town crier instead of instilled and percolated through Spanish sources. The King had been told by some ferreting churchmen that the marriage between him and the Queen was damnable, and it was said he was going to put her aside.

Only the people could not believe he would ever carry out so wicked a project. But the Spanish ambassador noted sadly they had no leader to guide them: "So this people will probably content themselves with only grumbling." He knew the English.

Henry's conscience might be arbitrary but it was none the less genuine. He did not think he was right, he knew he was. Twinges of conscience, stirrings of doubts or of remorse, never troubled him as they did those of lesser breed. It was not to justify himself to himself that he hounded the Pope and never yielded until he had achieved his ends. The supreme egotist who has never been countered feels no need of self-justification. It was to prove to the world he was right and anyone who thought the contrary was wrong.

Unlike Henry, Katherine refused to accept that they had been living in sin: they were bound as husband and wife in holy matrimony. To believe otherwise would imperil her immortal soul. And nothing would make her change her mind, even Henry. This lack of accommodation on her part came as an unpleasant surprise to him; he did not realize that Katherine might and did look upon him as her husband, king and lord, but never God.

She had not offended, but she believed the King's wish to separate from her was a judgement of God because her marriage to his elder brother had been sealed by innocent blood. Throughout the years she had been haunted by the memory of the young Earl of Warwick, and had always treated his sister tenderly. The sword had swept for him at her father's behest only because of his royal lineage: King Ferdinand had refused to fulfil her marriage contract until a potential rival of the Prince of Wales was removed—the dead could not usurp. There were some who believed Henry VIII's sonlessness was God's punishment for his father's action that November day on Tower Hill.

Only the Pope could grant a dispensation to annul their marriage; therefore everything depended on the Pope as far as the King and Queen of England were concerned. The new pontiff was an unknown quantity, but surely, Katherine prayed, no Vicar of Christ would annul a marriage a predecessor had legalized and blessed.

The lurid news that Rome had been sacked by the Emperor's troops who had taken the Pope prisoner spread like conflagration through Christendom. The very ground on which the Church stood crumbled beneath it. When horror reached saturation point and had to subside, one fact stood out stark as a solitary landmark on an otherwise riven landscape. No Pope would grant the King of England a divorce from his Spanish wife when he was a prisoner of the Spanish wife's nephew. Clement might be allowed to sit on St. Peter's chair, but it would not be his voice that would pronounce edicts, mandates and dispensations. It would be the Emperor's.

More than ever was Katherine sure that Wolsey was at the foot of everything when she heard he was going to France. She blamed him in the first instance for sowing in 'Henry's mind the seeds of separation from her. Now he was going to promote the King's marriage with a French princess. He was the originator, author and founder of the alliance with France; but for him, she was certain Henry would still be aligned to her nephew, whom Wolsey blamed for losing him the papal throne. England itself had no friendly disposition towards its hereditary enemy, and the engagement of Princess Mary that year to the French King's son roused no popular enthusiasm. The French envoys appraised the Dauphin's future bride very much as a farmer appraises stock—they might admire her conversation and looks, but she was so thin, spare and small, they said with some irritation, it would be impossible for her to be married for at least three years.

It was imperative for Wolsey to go to France; the

100

necessity was driven home to him—only he could achieve what was to be done. He had to enlist the aid of Francis to force Charles to release the Pope, otherwise the Pope could not supply the annulment for the King. And he had to prepare for the King's marriage, once he was free, to the Duchess of Alençon, sister of Francis.

He had no suspicion when he left England that the King intended to make Anne Boleyn his queen, no suspicion at all. How could he have, when her father was on a mission to France at the same time, to bring back the Duchess of Alençon's picture to show her future royal bridegroom? He never dreamt his expedition to France was a ruse by his enemies, headed by the Boleyn faction, to get him out of the country. That spring the hate between Norfolk and Wolsey had flashed into high words in front of the King himself. The aristocrat loathed the Cardinal not for what he was but for what he had sprung from. One day, he promised himself, he would eat that butcher's cur alive.

On his return, Wolsey rode post-haste to Richmond to tell the King he had brought back a firm alliance with France. He did not find his sovereign alone; Anne Boleyn was with him. It was she who spoke to his messenger, not the King: "Where else should the Cardinal come? Tell him to come here, where the King is."

As the tall Cardinal bowed his way backwards from their presence, he realized that if the King married Anne Boleyn exactly the same impediment stood between them as existed between him and Katherine. Katherine had been his brother's wife before she had been his; the King had been intimate with Anne Boleyn's sister, and the fact that it was illicit made it no less an impediment. That meant the Pope would have to be asked to make Katherine and the King's union unlawful and for the same reason make the King's union with Anne Boleyn lawful. It seemed a lot to ask, but Wolsey, who knew the ways of popes, did not doubt it could be done—once Clement was freed to do it.

Not a French princess to unite England and France for all time, their son and heir to be king of both countries, make them a power in the world strong enough, united enough to stand up to any emperor. The place of Katherine of Aragon, daughter of a Spanish king and Castilian queen, to be taken not by a princess of royal blood but an insignificant lady-in-waiting. To make her marriage lawful to England's king, the whole complicated machinery of the Church to be set in motion. Trumpery like Anne Boleyn to be England's queen!

Never again was the old warm rapport between king and minister to be re-established; there was an artificiality, a straining after effect in this trio that had never marred the duet. He might supply Anne Boleyn with delicacies from his table; she found them more delectable than even from the King's, but he knew there was more tooth than sweetness behind her honeyed blandishments. He might receive a letter from her assuring him she could never repay him for the great pains and troubles he was taking on her behalf except by loving him, next to the King's Grace, above all creatures living, but he knew such words were penned only because he was the means by which she hoped to be made queen. If confirmation were needed, he found it in the postscript added by the King, trusting by Wolsey's diligency and vigilancy (with the assistance of Almighty God) shortly to be eased out of trouble. Shortly! Wolsey tried to buy Anne's patience with rich and goodly presents, and assuage the King's impatience by writing still another petitioning letter to the Pope.

London was stolidly behind Katherine; they loved her, and sorrowed for her that she had not borne an heir to the throne. Providence, not she, was responsible for that. When they learnt that her place might be taken by Anne Boleyn, they seethed with indignation. It did not matter to them that her mother had been of noble birth; they thought of her as Nan Bullen, the granddaughter of a mayor, one of themselves, a lady-in-waiting to supplant her mistress and their queen—had the King taken leave of his senses?

The Pope was nominally free again, but everyone knew he was in the hollow of the Emperor's hand. At once two English bishops were dispatched to Italy, to obtain from him a commission empowering Wolsey to pronounce Katherine's marriage null and void. It was made as plain to the Supreme Pontiff as Wolsey could make it that if he refused the King of England's demands, he would involve Wolsey, the safety of the country and the papal cause in England in complete ruin.

The prelates found a cowed Pope in bad lodgings: his Holiness admitted that captivity in Rome was better than liberty here. He cried easily, sighed a great deal and escaped out of every corner he was hemmed into by saying he must consult his advisers. Day after day the Englishmen returned to assail the Holy Father for four or five hours at a stretch with their king's matrimonial troubles, their foreign voices rough and rude with plain speaking.

First of all they had to put Clement right on one or two points: they discovered he actually thought their sovereign wanted an annulment because he had fallen in love with a lady of doubtful virtue! Not for anything under the sun, they assured His Holiness, would Cardinal Wolsey have allowed himself to be influenced except by the conviction of the insufficiency of the King's present marriage. They dwelt at length on the purity of the lady Anne's life, her constant virginity, her maidenly and womanly modesty, her soberness, humility, wisdom, finishing with a flourish on her apparent aptness to procreate children.

On top of this shambles, on top of the sack of Rome, on top of horror, destruction and the total loss of all papal territories, the King of England's "great matter". Why were they bringing it to him who had so much else of so much more moment to despoil him? They must know the Emperor was breathing down his back. Why did the King of England not have two wives? A precedent could always be found in handy papal archives—dispensation granted to Henry IV of Castille to marry a second wife on condition that, if within a fixed time he had no issue by her, he should return to his first. Why could Queen Katherine not retire into a nunnery? That would involve injury to only one person, herself. When she refused to be agreeable, he wished her in her grave. Why, oh why, could the King of England not settle the matter for himself, as his brother-in-law Charles Brandon had done—obtain a divorce from the English courts and marry a second wife? All the Pope would be called upon to settle then would be validity of the second marriage, a comparatively easy matter after it was an accomplished fact.

Henry, however, was as determined to make the Pope shoulder his responsibilities as the Pope was anxious not to accept them. The King of England must have a sentence that would ensure the legitimacy of his children by the second marriage. The world must be shown the King of England's second marriage was unassailable. Only the Pope, whose decrees were the laws of the Church, could supply the necessary warrant.

It took more than one English commission to wring from him permission for Wolsey and (to give the proceedings an impartial air) the Italian Cardinal Campeggio to try the King's case in England and pronounce sentence. Either Cardinal might act by himself, and all appeals from their jurisdiction were forbidden. The Pope secretly bound himself not to revoke the case and gave a written promise he would confirm the Cardinals' decision.

The two English bishops returned to England with their

good tidings, which they carried to Greenwich. Princess Mary and some of her attendants were ill with smallpox, so Anne Boleyn had found temporary lodging in the tilt-yard to be out of infection's way. She was enraptured with the news, and as grateful as though they had brought the papal dispensation with them in their pockets. The King was as delighted, now things really were moving. Cardinal Campeggio was no stranger to England, a man after Henry's heart, a great canonist who knew the law. It was satisfactory to reflect that some years ago Henry had conferred upon him the bishopric of Salisbury, that the temporalities and revenues from the English diocese must mean a great deal to an Italian whose house had been looted and who had lost all his possession in the sack of Rome.

The firm alliance Wolsey had brought back from France included a joint declaration against the Emperor. The people in England woke up one day in January to find they were at war with their best customer—Flanders. Bales of cloth deteriorated on London wharves waiting to be shipped abroad. Trade dried up as looms clacked to a standstill. Merchants would not buy wool they could not sell to clothiers who had lost their markets. Workmen were dismissed, shops closed. There was revolt in Norfolk, rising in Wiltshire, the clothiers of Kent were all for seizing Wolsey and turning him adrift in a boat with holes bored in it.

Because war spelt ruin to the most prosperous industry in both England and Flanders, Henry and Charles began to discuss peace before hostilities actually took place and between them they reached a unique gentlemen's agreement: trade with Flanders was to go on as if there were no war. Thus it petered into a truce, leaving in its trail on the English side a gathering hatred against the Cardinal.

The dismal weather that spring foreboded the return of the dread sweating sickness. Henry made will after will, shared her devotions with Katherine and wrote love letters to Anne. The epidemic took its doleful toll, snatching the King's twelve-year-old nephew, only son of his sister Mary.

It was a blow from which Mary never recovered. She retired with her two daughters into the country where she who signed herself Mary the French Queen reigned sweetly and simply as lady of the manor. Her days of dancing youth had long since passed: if one of her husband's previous wives was not making claims, the other one was sure to be. She saw little of him in the years to come, for he was always at court, taking a masterful hand in the affairs of state, bearing the sceptre at a new queen's coronation, escorting another one to the Tower. He long survived his royal bride, the big rugged body stoutly weathering the years, into which he seemed to shrink a little, like the occupant of a family house only tenanting a few rooms.

With the Italian Legate on his way from Rome to pronounce his marriage to Katherine null, Henry had deemed it wise to silence the tittle-tattle regarding his favourite by sending Anne from court. She took her demission hardly and "smoked" over it in her father's house, refusing to return when permission was granted. This absenting of herself and making herself precious had the effect of greatly increasing the King's ardour, and he rode to visit her through the summer days, sounding his bugle when he came to a certain hill-top to tell her of his approach. It was to be a further three years before she consented to give herself to him.

As spring in England that year wasted into a barren summer, Cardinal Lorenzo Campeggio was arduously making from Italy to England. Crippled with gout, his journey was slow and painful: it was a physical impossibility for him to come with the haste his fellow Cardinal kept importuning for, and every stage of the way took toll of the pain-ridden traveller. Not until October did he reach England, his mandate from the Holy See stamped on his upright mind: to do his utmost to restore mutual affection between the King and Queen, not to proceed to sentence, and—the Church's unfailing nostrum—to protract the matter as long as possible.

He had to be borne in a litter for he was too weak to ride. Gnarled with disease, he was like one of those old trees whose knurrs and knots make it look as though it is growing upside down, its roots uppermost. As he swayed by on the road to London, women sprang up in his path, hurling at him acclamations for Queen Katherine and shouting, their voices violent with warning, "No Nan Bullen for us!"

CHAPTER TEN

TRIAL OF A QUEEN

"Cold, alter'd friends, with cruel art,
Poisoning fell Misfortune's dart."

THE Italian found it impossible to impress the Pope's point of view on his fellow Cardinal; he had no more success in persuading Wolsey than if he had spoken to a rock. Wolsey's objections were founded on the invalidity of the marriage, the instability of the realm and the succession. It was driven home to Campeggio that the King would brook no procrastination; the affairs of the kingdom were at a standstill, and the cause dare not remain undetermined any longer.

The Englishman's vehemence startled the Italian: the King must have his annulment which the Pope must supply, otherwise where would Wolsey stand and what would happen to the Papacy in England? Industriously Campeggio reported to Rome that the Cardinal of York was certainly proving himself very zealous for the preservation of the See Apostolic in England, adding with one of those flashes of penetration of which the single-minded are capable, "because all his grandeur is connected with it".

Unable to ride or walk, he was carried to have audience with the King. Here was no English prelate eager to implement his sovereign's most difficult demand smoothly for him, but a fleshless Italian earnest with another opinion.

If Campeggio found himself against a rock when he spoke to Wolsey, he wrote that not even an angel in heaven could turn the King from his own interpretation of the facts. The English monarch listened patiently enough, but in reply trotted out all the arguments he had already heard from Wolsey. The King was word perfect as the dictums and axioms originated from him in the first place.

Only when Campeggio suggested the Queen might be persuaded to enter a religious house did the atmosphere lighten. The King became cheerful at once: that would be the solution to everything. After all, Katherine had always been devout, and even when the court was at its gayest had denied herself and observed vigils. Now he had ceased cohabiting with her and would never return to her bed, a nunnery was surely the most appropriate place for her to end her days. If she agreed, he would be prepared to be most generous, would even settle the succession on her daughter should he fail to have sons by another marriage. No time must be lost, and it was arranged Wolsey and Campeggio should repair the very next day with this most fruitful suggestion to his consort.

Katherine had been born in camp when her mother's forces were beleaguering Granada. She had been brought up amidst battles and siege, and she did not succumb when faced by two Cardinals. In all the shabby business with its sordid dissembling and specious argument, she stands out with a nobility that still reaches and touches us.

Wolsey cannot have felt comfortable or happy in her presence, but he was at such a desperate pass that in all probability exigency forestalled every other emotion.

We do know that Katherine concentrated on the Italian rather than the English Cardinal.

She nonplussed them both by saying she had heard they were to come to induce her to enter a religious house. Both pictured for her the advantages of a nunnery. She would have everything to gain and nothing to lose by taking such a step—her dower and the guardianship of her daughter. She was reminded of the first wife of Louis XII of France who still lived in the greatest honour and reputation with God and all that kingdom. Katherine listened with her customary courtesy, but they were talking to a woman who did not believe she could accommodate her immortal soul.

One dark winter's morning Wolsey wakened Campeggio at daybreak with the news the Queen was asking leave to confess to him. Gone like a summer day never to return were the times he, Wolsey, Archbishop of York, had acted as confessor and confidant to his sovereign lady. For a lifetime he had played second fiddle to one alone and that was the King; everyone else had had to dance to his tune. Now he found himself taking second place to an Italian twisted with pain, impoverishd to beggary after being forced to redeem his life at a great sum by the vandals who sacked Rome.

Henry found Katherine indestructible as an adversary. She had nothing to hide, and the very simplicity of her case could stand the broad glare of daylight. That was why, like the Pope, he often wished her dead, not so much that death would silence her but that only death could bring his great matter to a conclusion no one could gainsay.

She came early that morning to the Italian Legate and spent a long time with him. What she told him was under the seal of confession but she granted him permission to repeat it and to write certain resolutions to the Pope. "She affirmed on her conscience that from her marriage with Prince Arthur on the 14th November, until his death on the 2nd April, she had not slept with him more than seven nights, and that he had left her as he had found her—a virgin." Instead of entering a religious house, she intended to live and die in the state of matrimony to which God had called her—"that she would always remain of that opinion and never change it." Her words had the ominous ring of an ultimatum, and ultimatums were the prerogatives of her husband, not his wife.

Campeggio received the Queen's statements on her union with the Prince of Wales gratefully: in his view they closed the door irrevocably on any marriage-suit case. Her husband must know if her words were true, as Campeggio was convinced they were. Then it did not matter whether the dispensation were valid or invalid; she was Henry VIII's wife and not the Prince of Wales's widow. Where was the point of holding an investigation when obviously there was nothing to investigate? But this Wolsey would not allow. Dexterously he elaborated argument after argument with his persuasive tongue. Rome was tired of the whole matter, but Wolsey dare not let Rome go. The King expected, the King had been led to believe the Pope would confirm the verdict the Legates reached in England: there must therefore be a court, a verdict and a confirmation.

The only way to deal with an indestructible adversary was to behave exactly as though she had no case, which, when Henry considered his own inviolate one, was a comparatively easy matter. Katherine could be spied on, mistreated, stripped of her interests and rights, her wishes ignored, all because the King knew his cause was just.

He summoned the Lord Mayor and his aldermen to his palace at Bridewell where he expounded to them, that they could declare it to the people of England, why there had to be a trial. Londoners had no love of or reverence for the Pope—Campeggio had seen ribald remarks about his master scrawled on the walls, and they had shrugged aside the sack of Rome with the comment that the Pope was a ruffian, unworthy of his place, who began the mischief and was well served.

Henry dwelt at length on the sores that vexed his mind. He harped back to the succession again and yet again—it must be ensured; compared the twenty years of peace and prosperity they had enjoyed during his reign with what their forebears had endured during the Wars of the Roses when the succession was in dispute. He extolled the Queen's many qualities—God's law and God's law alone stood in his way of continuing to live with so good a wife. He hoped the affair would be settled amicably—that was their affable monarch they knew so well who was speaking. But if he "found anyone, whoever he was, who spoke in any terms than he aught to do of his Prince, he would let him know that he was his master". His audience sighed and said nothing. "Never a head so dignified but that he would make it fly". He meant that, every word of it, bluff King Hal.

The curious thing was, despite being made the King's confidants, despite no heir to the throne, the people still backed the Queen. It was she London championed, not the King. Henry had never envisaged such a situation, and it outraged him. His council mirrored his hurt feelings by expressing as their own that the Queen was acting contrary to her temper and ordinary behaviour, showing herself much abroad, and by civilities and gracious bowings of her head (which was not her custom formerly) seeking to work upon the affections of the people. The Queen, however, had the affections of the people, particularly the women, without any working upon them. Throughout the whole proceedings she acted in character, and it was this endowment that lent her dignity sweetness and spiritual power.

Meanwhile the King had lodged her rival in a fine house near to his own, hoping in this way so to accustom his subjects to her they would begin to take her for granted. The French ambassador busily reported to his government the King was so infatuated God alone could abate his madness. He noted more homage was paid to her than *she* ever paid the Queen: she had her ladies-in-waiting, her train-bearer, her chaplains, and courtiers flocked round the favourite who dispensed patronage as though she already wore the crown. Anne had staked her claim; she must have all or nothing, and the King, who signed his letters to her "Your loyal and most assured servant," made no secret that she was to have all.

He wrote her a very short note before she was installed in her new house, found through the offices of the indefatigable Wolsey, in which he takes her to task very kindly. He remarks that what he was writing to her was being circulated in London, at which he marvelled not a little. Lack of discreet handling alone could be the cause: he meant Anne's overtalkative tongue. The note is signed, "Written with the hand of him that longeth to be yours, H.R." A volatile temperament such as hers readily betrayed her into indiscretions. That is why her cool and calculating handling of her royal lover proves that where he was concerned she was ruled by her head and not her heart.

The King was entering his thirty-eighth year and the new Venetian ambassador was as rapturous over his appearance as any of his predecessors had been when he was much younger. Such corporal and intellectual beauty in "this Eighth Henry" not merely surprised but astounded. "His face is angelic rather than handsome; his head imperial and bold." But for the first time Henry's magnificent physique revealed its human origin rather than the god-like immunity which had protected it heretofore. He began to suffer from incapacitating headaches: in one of his letters to Anne he mentions the pain in his head after spending more than four hours of that day writing his book in defence of the dissolution of his marriage. Henry was nothing if not literate.

The weeks of the new year teased themselves into months as new deputations were sent from England to the Pope. His Holiness was asked to declare as forgery a providential brief Katherine's party had unearthed which removed any doubts about the earlier dispensation. The Queen had suggested both she and her husband should take monastic vows—would Clement dispense with the vows in the King's case but not the Queen's?

His Holiness began to show every indication of irritation at the King's great matter not being allowed to settle on its lees. Henry was the two horns of his dilemma. At one meeting he forbade the English delegate to proceed and, growing more angry and more excited, said he would make no further concessions. Obviously the Pope was prepared to do nothing for the King's Grace; indeed there was talk in Rome that the Emperor had commanded Clement to recall the Legatine commission. The delegation returned promptly to England—the trial must go forward with expedition before the Pope could interfere.

It opened in London, in the great hall of the Black Friars, on the last day of May, 1529, the trial to determine the validity of the marriage of Henry VIII to Katherine of Aragon, which the Legates were to decide and the Pope to confirm.

Every day the court sat the two Legates were there, sitting "in a solemn place", before an empty railed table covered with carpets and tapestry. They entered behind "crosses, pillars, axes, and all ceremonies belonging to their degree". On the right, under a cloth of estate, was a chair and cushions for the King when he was present, on the left a chair on a lower level for the Queen. Council for the King and Queen faced each other on opposite sides. The Archbishop of Canterbury and all the bishops of the realm sat in a semicircle before the Legates. Officers of the court, proctors, the lords temporal, ladies and friends of the court, witnesses filled the body of the great hall with restlessness like palpitation.

In his chair covered with cloth of gold sat Wolsey, Cardinal of York, next his fellow Legate. If ever there was a stickler for the law it was Cardinal Campeggio. Not one jot nor one tittle was allowed to pass, not that all should be fulfilled but, it seemed to his colleague, to protract the proceedings indefinitely. The only occasions the tedium of the sessions was broken were when the King graced the court with his presence.

Both he and the Queen were there on the 21st June, the first and only time they were present on the same day. She arrived first, then the King made his entrance. The atmosphere was charged to explosion point. The King rose and harangued the court, telling it he was determined to live no longer in sin with his wife the Queen. The legality of the marriage which pained his conscience must be decided speedily; therefore he required the Legates to proceed at once.

Wolsey reminded the court that the case had been committed to him and his colleague by the Pope. He promised he would render judgement to the best of his poor ability and "omit nothing that the justice of the case required".

Now it was the Queen's turn. She did not address the court as she had done previously, she addressed the King. She had to make her way amongst the crowded assemblage until she reached his chair, where she knelt at his feet.

"Sir," she began, "I beseech you for all the loves that

hath been between us, and for the love of God, let me have justice and right, take of me some pity and compassion, for I am a poor woman and a stranger born out of your dominion. I have here no assured friend, and much less indifferent counsel. I flee to you as to the head of justice within this realm."

It was he who had taught her to speak English, but she had always spoken it with a broken accent. Today it made her sound very much a foreigner.

"I take God and all the world to witness, that I have been to you a true, humble and obedient wife, ever conformable to your will and pleasure; I loved all those you loved, only for your sake, whether they were my friends or mine enemies."

She had not always been as she was now, small, broad and moving like a column, but that was what she was now.

"This twenty years I have been your true wife, and by me ye have had divers children, although it hath pleased God to call them out of this world, which has been no fault of mine."

They rose before him, a ghostly small train, the first little dead daughter, the son he had held in his arms who was to secure the succession for all time, the boy he had never seen born to him between the victories in France and of Flodden, the baby fleetingly referred to as "the King's new son" who lived only long enough to be christened, the miscarriages, the premature births—every one proved the wrath of Omnipotent God. Only Mary had He allowed, Mary who was a daughter, not an heir.

"And when ye had me at the first, I take God to be my judge, I was a true maid without touch of man; and whether it be true or no, I put it to your conscience."

His conscience. God had turned His face from their union. Henry dare not fly in the teeth of His manifest

116

displeasure any longer. That was what his conscience told him. The succession must be assured.

Twice he raised his kneeling wife. She questioned the validity of the court and on the words "To God I commit my cause!" she made a low obeisance to the King. Then leaning on the arm of her receiver-general, she left the court instead of resuming her seat.

"Madam," her attendant whispered to her, "you are called back."

"I hear it well enough," she answered as the crier's summons rang after her, "Katherine, Queen of England, come again into the court." "But on—on, go you on, for this is no court wherein I can have justice. Proceed, therefore." She had not gone more than a few steps before she said, more to herself than to him, "I never before disputed the will of my husband, and I shall take the first opportunity to ask pardon for my disobedience."

"She is, my lords," said her affected husband, "as true, as obedient, and as conformable a wife as I could, in my fantasy, wish or desire. She has all the virtuous qualities that ought to be in a woman of her dignity, or in any other of baser estate."

Outside, waiting for her, were the women of London. They shouted their encouragement to her, telling her to care for nothing and not to give in to her enemies. If the matter were to be decided by the women, the French ambassador reported, the King would lose the battle.

But the matter was to be decided by men, by two Legates hearing legal argument, and witnesses brought forward to substantiate the King's case that Queen Katherine was not a virgin when she came to his bed. Twenty-five years they went back to a boy bridegroom who boasted, "I have been this night in the midst of Spain." Fifteen was the Prince of Wales? The Earl of Shrewsbury attested he had known his wife before he was sixteen. The Duke of Norfolk remembered Prince Arthur was of good complexion and nature and above fifteen—of course he carnally knew his lady—did not the speaker himself at the same age know and carnally use a woman? "They may do whatever they like," Campeggio wrote to Rome, "and conduct the trial with all those arts which can influence the results in their favour."

Not quite as they liked. One man "stood stiff in the Queen's cause": John Fisher, Bishop of Rochester, whose robes hung on a body lean with abstinence and penance, upright and tall as a tree. There he stood, saying, since the King sought to know the truth, John Fisher would be glad to tell him. He presented himself before their reverend lordships to assert and demonstrate with cogent reasons that this marriage of the King and Queen could not be dissolved by any power, divine or human. In maintenance of this he was willing to lay down his life. As a gesture of confirmation of all he had spoken, he handed the Legates the copy of a book he had written on the subject.

His flailing words caught Wolsey on the raw, but he was never at a loss for a reply. In the stunned silence he protested against this attack on the Legates. The court had been called to hear the case and render judgement in whatever way divine wisdom should incline them so to do. How dare the Bishop of Rochester take upon himself by the positiveness and vigour of his utterance to pre-empt the prerogative of the court and pronounce judgement himself!

His fellow Legate said nothing, but from the moment John Fisher, like the knuckle-bone of God, made his stand, he, Lorenzo Campeggio, was different. The Cardinal of York—everyone—marked the change, wondering what it betokened. Instead of with precision, he acted now like a man who had the courage to come to decision.

On the 23rd July the King's Grace was present to hear

the ruling in his favour. After the preliminary lengthy perorations his counsel at the bar called fast for judgement, and Cardinal Campeggio rose to pronounce it.

In the fluent Latin of the scholar which his audience could all understand, he said it was the custom of the court in Rome to suspend all legal proceedings from the end of July until the commencement of October. "I shall wade no further in this matter, unless I have the just opinion and judgement, with the assent of the Pope, of such other of his counsel as hath more experience and learning in such doubtful laws as I have. Wherefore I will adjourn this court for this time, according to the order of the court in Rome, from whence this court and jurisdiction is derived."

He had obeyed the secret instructions of his master to settle the case without pronouncing sentence. It was a moment or two before the full import of his words reached his hearers, as they adjusted themselves to believe the unbelievable. Instead of sentence adjournment, instead of pronouncement in the King's favour, nothing at all.

Noisily Henry rose. He and his cause had been held up to ridicule before England, before the world. In that hall, stale with reaction as if death had taken place, his every movement sounded as if he were an army in full battle array. He clattered from the court.

The scene was not played out. There was still another actor to say his part, a principal player who could redeem the piece. The commission wrung from the Pope provided either Cardinal could act by himself. Now was the turn of Campeggio's colleague to retrieve the situation and declare for his King.

He rose, his ageing face grey with fatigue, and seconded his fellow Legate. "We be but commissioners for a time, and can, or may not, by virtue of our commission, proceed to judgement without the knowledge and consent of the chief head of our authority, and having his consent to the same; which is the Pope."

At the end of the road, when it came to the parting of the ways, Thomas Cardinal Wolsey enlisted on the side of the Church and forsook his sovereign lord. He needed no archbishop to whisper in his ear that to provoke the wrath of a king spelt death.

CHAPTER ELEVEN

DEATH OF THE CARDINAL

"K was a King, so mighty and grand,
L was a Lady, who had a white hand."

HENRY had reached a watershed in his life; he had reigned
for twenty years and was to reign for a further eighteen.
The first twenty had been coloured by the brilliant personality of his chief minister, Thomas Wolsey, the latter
eighteen were to be stamped by the character and will of
the King himself. With Wolsey went spectacle and the
spectacular, with the King came government and rule.
The difference between the two men was the difference
between personality and character: the King was what
Wolsey was not, a realist. His development was not so
much a matter of slow growth, rather a succession of
gigantic starts that rounded themselves into finality, like
the mounds a mole throws up. His continuity was a
channelling more than roots, painful as these can be, and
so finally he undermined himself as a man.

He used Parliament to shape his ends. Never before in
the annals of England had Parliament met so often as it
did in the latter half of Henry's reign, and it was this

governing by consent that makes him great as a king. He did not distrust Parliament as Wolsey had done; he was not afraid of it as some of his predecessors had been. He might dominate it but he never attempted to intimidate it. Embedded in the statute-book for the last eighteen years of his reign are acts and laws which mark a turning point in English history and which have never been equalled.

He was learning also how to master himself, to curb a temper that could have betrayed a lesser man into bouts of violence. His passions were strong but he kept them well bridled, his manners were invariably good even under the most trying circumstances, and above all he knew how to keep himself to himself. "Three may keep counsel if two be away," he was wont to say; "and if I thought my cap knew my counsel, I would cast it in the fire and burn it." This concealment of his thoughts and intentions was what made him so terrifying as he grew older: no one knew until sentence fell how long one had been at the bar, and there was neither reprieve nor pity from the judge who sat in isolation in that uncapped head.

The difficulty of procuring an annulment, which he had thought would be simple, undoubtedly hardened him, and much of his pleasantness receded before the steeling and strengthening of his will. But that was in the years to come; the blood still ran warm in his veins, and he still had affection for the man who had been his chief minister. It was Anne Boleyn, made vindictive by disappointment, to whom Wolsey attributed his downfall. "I know there is a night crow that possesses the royal ear against me, and misrepresents all my actions."

The Duke of Norfolk had the exquisite pleasure of demanding from the butcher's cur the Great Seal of England, but this my lord of York refused to deliver until he saw the King's signature. Back next day rode Norfolk with the Master of the Rolls and letters from the King. The surrender of the seals, on St. Luke's Day, toppled the Cardinal from his lofty pinnacle. He was required to give up to the King the great palaces he had built at York Place and Hampton Court, his property and estates, and all his goods. Seldom had such an accumulation of riches been displayed: plate of silver and gold, cloths of all colours including a thousand pieces of fine holland, and vestments the like of which had never before been seen in England.

London assembled in its thousands at the water's edge and took boat to catch a nearer view, to watch the stricken Cardinal being taken to the Tower. The pomp, panoply and parade with which he used to ride through the city had all diminished to a barge, rocking on the tide. Here he came, with only a single cross borne before him this time, that of York.

That was not—that could not be the Cardinal. Had they not seen him often enough to tell him at a glance? But that was he, all right, the cross told you that, and the redness of his robes; only his face had dwindled to half its size; like a finger-nail it looked.

He must know what was awaiting him at the Tower, they all knew what was awaiting him. All that display of pride and power come to this. He must have been about the richest man in England—that was one thing church-men knew better than their paternoster, how to amass and keep wealth. They were all the same, every single one of the Pope's men, with the priest refusing to bury your dead until you had paid the last penny of what he claimed as his fee. Bare of bed and board the Cardinal would find the Tower after the opulence of his palaces. A great man he had been, firm with substance; and now you were going to watch him, old and shaken, slipping past you on the way to prison in his red robes, the only thing he had left.

But the barge was not heading for the Tower, it was moving in the other direction. What did that mean, think you? Only one thing: he wasn't being carried through Traitors' Gate, so you could wait here long enough for he was not going to pass. The King must still be behind him then, or it would have been the wind in his teeth for him.

The Cardinal went to Esher Palace, a subsidiary old house to new Hampton Court. Both had belonged to him in the past, both now were the King's like everything else in his one-time possession, but his royal master allowed his old servant to tenant it in the meantime.

Here Thomas Wolsey waited, feeding himself on secret messages from his sovereign to be patient. Others sat where he had sat, filled offices he had filled, handled affairs of state as he would not have handled them. The man praying in Esher for restoration to the King's favour did not realize his day was past, a day that encompassed an epoch. Never again would a cleric wield the power he had wielded; a lawyer now held the Great Seal in place of the priest. Never again would a servant of the crown, cleric or layman, possess the power he, Thomas Wolsey, had possessed.

He could not foresee in the shuffling of the cards, as posts were refilled and the insignia of authority changed hands, that there was one there who would become Pope in England with powers no Pope had ever possessed. He was not to know that the King with his boy's face had learnt from him the principle of one-man rule, and that the pupil was far to out-distance the master.

The first thing Henry did after the debacle of the Legates' court was to summon Parliament, which was the last thing his former minister would have done. It was an audacious move on his part, for the people, represented by Members of Parliament, were sympathetic towards Katherine and actively hostile to the woman whom he wished to supplant her. But nobody strengthened Henry's hand more than the Pope, whose bungling irresolution galvanized itself into the decisive step of maintaining that the King's case would not only have to be decided by Rome but in Rome.

Every Englishman, whoever he was, noble or yeoman, thought the same about that. Their King cited to appear in Rome! Who did this Pope think he was to publish such a decree? They would like to tell him if the King did go it would be at the head of an army. They had never liked the idea to begin with of their monarch summoned to plead in his own realm before an English and an Italian papal representative; even Katherine's sympathizers expressed resentment at their sovereign subjected to such a procedure. But cited to appear in person at a foreign court in a foreign land, with the Emperor's foreign spears bristling behind the papal throne! There was not a man in England who would have allowed such a thing, far less King Hal himself, thank God for that.

This harmony between sovereign and subject was what made it possible for Henry to achieve what he did. He understood the temper of his people, and they acquiesced in what he did because he and they were on the same side. For long a corrupt Church had lost its hold, and secularization spreads in a thriving commonalty. It might be a theological age, it was also an irreligious one. The Reformation did not come in England as it came in neighbouring Scotland, as it did to Germany and Switzerland, through men whose blazing heat to redress wrongs forged Protestantism. There was no John Knox in England, no Martin Luther or John Calvin. When the English Reformation came it came through the State and not a counter church, and the State was Henry VIII. Its impulse was not a matter of conscience but a grievance about money. It would have come about without the King's divorce; the wand of the arrow had been fashioning for some time as men disparaged the Church for its wealth, but the divorce was the goose's feather that winged it on its way.

Word was brought to Wolsey at Esher how the new Lord Chancellor had spoken of the King, who was present at the opening of Parliament, as the good, ever vigilant shepherd who, for the well-being of his flock, had recently thrust out "the great wether". He did not need to be told who was the great wether who had presumed the shepherd had no wit to perceive his crafty doing. Pitiable indeed had been his mistake, for his Grace's sight was so quick and penetrable he not only saw but saw through him, both within and without.

The Lords, after mustering forty-four charges against him, brought in a bill of attainder to make the Cardinal's reinstatement impossible. Only one man spoke in his defence, Thomas Cromwell, his one-time secretary, and he persuaded the Commons to reject the bill. Wolsey knew he must have acted with the King's connivance, or it would have been passed. His one link with his royal master in the days to come was this Cromwell, an up-and-coming man, not a butcher's but a blacksmith's son, who had been a trooper, a merchant and a money-lender in the past, and who carried the rigour of the soldier, the perspicacity of the trader and the tenacity of the money-lender into the present.

Parliament was informed that their vigilant shepherd wished to be released from the obligation to repay a loan which the great wether had raised for him. His flock did not allow the bill to pass without some opposition and final amendment. A member of London, one John Petit, rose and spoke against releasing the King from his debts to his people. There was no question of Henry treating him as an offender or ordering his arrest; genially he would ask the next time he was there if Petit were on his side. He was too secure in the saddle not to give Parliament rein, or to resort to pack it. No go-between was allowed to come between him and either of the Houses; his relation to both was more like that of an acting prime minister than spectator sovereign.

Measures were passed for reforming the clergy in which old grievances were redressed. Clergy were forbidden to hold more than one living, a priest was prohibited to keep a benefice unless he lived in it, and could be fined if he absented himself for more than a month. The people felt well served by Parliament. Poetic justice had been meted out to clerics who could no longer extort exorbitant dues and fees and could be fined themselves if they did not behave.

Henry was not so successful in his domestic women's world as he was with that of a man's Parliament. Instead of well on the way to marriage with the King and crowned as his queen, Anne found herself as far away as ever from her aims. Frustration made her waspish. She knew consciously now what she had always known unconsciously: that, despite his handsome presents and the flower of his compliments, the Cardinal despised her. She and her party were convinced it was not lack of skill that had failed to procure the Pope's annulment, but lack of will. Wolsey could if he would, and he had not.

She exacted full payment for her disappointment from Henry, charging him with the passing of her youth, putting a price on her honour and holding over his head the perpetual threat that she would go away. Her tears had the effect that a woman's tears do have on certain men. He felt he would go to almost any lengths to mollify her, abjectly entreating her not to leave him.

Katherine remained at court, his nominal wife, his more than nominal consort and queen, the woman whose life he had shared for twenty years, whom he had once loved and would always respect. She did not cry her eyes out in front of him, nonetheless he felt she was due some consideration. Man-like, he tried to please both in turn, and in his effort to make up to one for the other, heavily overplayed his hand with each.

That Christmas the thirteen-year-old Mary was at Greenwich to join the festivities with her father and mother. His small flaxen-haired daughter did not make the demands, tacit or otherwise, that his love and helpmeet made. He could lavish on her all the tenderness he felt without any sense of guilt. One would really think his bookworm of a daughter was the apple of his eye, not Anne.

Some contemporaries believed that Anne was Henry's mistress by this time; Wolsey obviously did with his night crow remark. They were certainly cohabiting eighteen months later. But in 1529, the year of the Legates' court, Henry's almost slavish attitude to her points to unfulfilled desire.

Anne Boleyn was small boned and this slenderness made her appear less tall than she was. Very tiny and very precious she seemed in the King's big arms, with her brown eyes and heart-shaped face. She was sprightly with intelligence and her beautiful mouth could say things that were clever and had an edge to them. She was not a good husbandwoman like Katherine; the King as well as gratuities and costly gifts and an indulgent income, was forever paying accounts for her from the privy purse for stuffs and furs, hunting gear that she could join in his sport, including a shooting-glove, wearing apparel, embroidery, everything a lady of fashion could desire.

The Cardinal was allowed to retain the rich archbishopric of York, and hopefully he set out for his See in spring. He had been appointed to it fifteen years ago but had never gone near it or taken the trouble to be installed. His enemies believed he, an absentee arch-priest, would be murdered by the people of his province, and were chagrined to learn he was quite well received. Their chagrin developed into distrust when they heard how

· ANNO · ÆTATIS ·   · SVÆ · XLIX ·

Henry VIII, aged forty-nine, painted by Holbein in the year he married
Anne of Cleves. In the Corsini Gallery, Rome

Henry VII, father of Henry VIII, holding the red rose of Lancaster. Painting by an unknown artist, reproduced by permission of the National Portrait Gallery

Elizabeth, wife of Henry VII and mother of Henry VIII, holding the white rose of York. Painting by an unknown artist, reproduced by permission of the National Portrait Gallery

Prince Arthur, the elder son, who married Katherine of Aragon and died at sixteen. After the painting in the Royal Collection, Windsor

Prince Henry, the younger son, when he was a child. From the painting in the collection of Sir Edmund and Lady Verney at Rhianva, Anglesey

Princess Margaret (identity uncertain), the elder daughter, headstrong and dominant. Painting by an unknown artist, reproduced by permission of the National Portrait Gallery

Princess Mary, Henry's favourite sister, the loveliest woman of her day. A painting of the French School, sixteenth century

Katherine of Aragon, Henry's first wife, mother of Mary Tudor. A painting by Michael Sittow, reproduced by permission of the Kunsthistorischen Museum, Vienna

Anne Boleyn, Henry's second wife whom he described as "my great folly"; mother of Elizabeth Tudor. Painting by an unknown artist, reproduced by permission of the National Portrait Gallery

Jane Seymour, Henry's third wife, mother of his only legitimate son, Edward Tudor. Brown Brothers.

Anne of Cleves, Henry's fourth wife. A painting in St. John's College, Oxford

Katherine Howard, Henry's fifth and youngest wife, said to be the loveliest of all his brides. After a miniature by Holbein in the Royal Collection

Katherine Parr, Henry's sixth and last wife. An engraving from a painting by Adrian van der Werff

Henry VIII arriving at the Field of the Cloth of Gold.
After a contemporary painting at Hampton Court

Henry with his three children, Edward, Mary and Elizabeth, all of whom reigned. An engraving by F. Bartolozzi from the original by Holbein at Ditton Park

Edward, Henry's beloved son, known as England's Treasure. A chalk and water-colour drawing by Holbein, reproduced by permission of the Kupferstichkabinett, Basel

Charles Brandon, Henry's closest lifelong friend who married Princess Mary

Thomas Wolsey, Cardinal of York, with the college he founded at Oxford in the background. From the original by Holbein in the collection at Christ Church, Oxford

humbly the Cardinal had entered on his pastoral duties, winning not only respect and praise from his flock but their love. Would York, a great way off, contain their old enemy? They did not believe it would.

Many men were administering what once one alone had controlled. The King burst forth at his council that the Cardinal was a better man than any of them at managing matters to his liking. They feared Wolsey more after his fall than they had in his pride. This man's goose would have to be cooked once and for all before it was too late.

On the 1st November, on the eve of his belated enthronement, when Wolsey was sitting at dinner with his chaplains, a strong party of horsemen rode into the courtyard. It was led by the young Earl of Northumberland whom the Cardinal knew well, for he had been in his service to be trained in the way he should go when he was Lord Percy. Was that only seven short years ago? How time slackened and contracted with the using of it. When the Earl had been Henry Percy, the Cardinal had broken at the King's command his love-troth with Anne Boleyn. A spirited defence he had put up of the girl with whom he had tangled and ensured himself. Even after his father had been brought from the north to tell him roundly to do as he was bid, he had argued and objected until forced to renounce his word.

Here he was, young Henry Percy, who had stepped into his father's shoes since then and one of the worthiest earldoms in the kingdom, being greeted by his old master on All Saints as though his visit at that hour with so many attendants was natural and expected.

Pretending not to notice his one-time pupil was trembling with agitation, the Cardinal took him into his bedchamber that he might put off his riding apparel, talking all the time like the good host he was to make his guest at ease. Immediately they were shut off from attendants, servants and chaplains, Wolsey snapped silent. In silence the young man and the old walked to the window, when the Cardinal felt his companion's hand placed lightly on his arm.

"My lord, I arrest you of high treason."

The gifts, messages and tokens from the King since his demission were all obliterated by words spoken faint as a whisper. The protection of the royal shadow no longer hovered over him. Wolsey knew what lay before him: the Tower, trial and certain death. He left York with the noise of his parishioners reverberating in his ears, "God save your Grace!" "God save your Grace!" "The foul evil take all them that take you from us!"

God did save his grace. Suffering from a cruel internal complaint, he died on his way to London in Leicester Abbey. The monks reverently clothed the long narrow bones in the full robes and regalia of his office, and laid him to rest. "If I had served God as diligently as I have done the King," he sighed on his death-bed, "He would not have given me over in my grey hairs."

After his death, Henry had neither the compunction nor regret for his former chancellor that he had felt during his lifetime. It was as though the memory of his old servant was not only sponged from his mind but must be ground from the records. He erected his own coats of arms wherever he could on Wolsey's palaces and renamed after himself Cardinal College, which had been the dead man's joy and pride to build at Oxford.

If the King had to come and go with Parliament, he found he could ride roughshod over the Lords spiritual. Except for Fisher, there was not one of the heroic mould that makes for martyrdom. The Archbishop of Canterbury, the highest dignitary in England, was a man mild to timidity, who would accept bad lest a worst thing befall him. In the past when Church and sovereign clashed, the Church had been stronger than king. Sure of its own ground, the line of demarcation across which royal prerogative dare not penetrate was jealously guarded. In Henry's time there was no line—as he found.

He demanded to be recognized as sole protector and "Supreme Head of the Church and clergy of England". The prelates were horrified at a title that diminished papal supremacy, but the Archbishop was even more horrified at the thought of the royal displeasure, and nothing is more contagious than fear. When he proposed the new title for their sovereign, with the meaningless rider "as far as the law of Christ allows", he added weakly, "Silence gives consent." "Then are we all silent," cried the clergy.

Henry had his way; whatever opposition he might have to encounter in the future, he knew it would not come from the Church in his own land.

Reinforced with new ammunition, he returned to his assault on the entrenched See of Rome. Politely he wrote to Clement, taking some pains to make it clear to the Vicar of Christ that he, the King of England, was only head of the Church in England. Once more the Pope was requested to annul his marriage. Should he fail to do so, Henry, using the royal we, pointed out, "Our condition will not be wholly irremediable. Extreme remedies are ever harsh of application; but he that is sick will by all means be rid of his distemper." His Holiness had been warned.

CHAPTER TWELVE

MATTERS OF CONSCIENCE

" 'Ye are my jewel, and only ane,
    Nane's do you injury;
For ere this-day-month come and gang
    My wedded wife ye'se be.' "

KATHERINE and Anne were like two rival queen bees in
the hive of the court; when the elder woman took her
customary place, the younger did not appear, and when
the younger queened it at a banquet given by the King in
her honour, the elder was absent. There was no inter-
mingling of their trains; only the dominant males remained the same.

Henry did not open the divorce question directly with
Katherine after the first occasion when the ominous news
was broken to her they had been living in sin all their
married lives. If she had to be approached on the subject,
a delegation prompted by the King was appointed to put
before her still another proposal amplified by his views.
So that when they met, and dined side by side, there
appeared on the face of things nothing different in the
pattern of their lives.

Yet to Henry nothing was the same. Instead of the one to exert pressure, he for the first time in his life became the object feeling it. Anne, now sure of her hold on him, became more and more tyrannical until he complained to her uncle Norfolk that she was not like the Queen, who never in her life used ill words to him.

He could boast, and mean it, that if the Pope issued ten thousand excommunications he would not care a straw for them; that he was King, Emperor and Pope all in one so far as his own country was concerned. But there were uneasy rumours that Charles was preparing for war in defence of his aunt. Hostilities involved money for arms as well as the loss of England's best customer, and Parliament showed no enthusiasm for either consequence. The House fairly buzzed with accord when one Member rose to move that their sovereign should take back the Queen to wife and thus solve both problems.

The last deputation sent to attend on Katherine before the separation was large and imposing, but neither its numbers nor the importance of its personages could persuade her to withdraw her suit from Rome. To her the Pope was the mirror image of eternal Truth, and he alone could judge. She would not consider the case being placed before four English prelates and four English nobles, even when reminded once again of the King's troubled conscience crying out for settlement. "God grant my husband a quiet conscience," was her reply, "but I mean to abide by no decision excepting that of Rome."

A fortnight later Henry and Anne rode together from Windsor Castle as they had ridden often enough in the past, but this time they did not return. Katherine received no warning; man-like Henry could not bring himself to say good-bye. He sent instructions that she must move from Windsor to one of Wolsey's old houses, where she took up residence with a small household. "Go where I may," she said, "I am his wife, and for him will

133

I pray." She blamed her former lady-in-waiting for edging him into heresy and disobedience to Rome. Anne and her father were described as more Lutheran than Luther; it was not, however, devotion to the Gospel which made them "true apostles of the new sect" but because the Pope had failed to produce the annulment.

Katherine never saw her husband again, nor her daughter who was parted from her about the same time. There is a pathetic item in the royal accounts, a payment by the King to Dr. Butts of a considerable sum for attending to his daughter Mary: the entry is dated the same month that he separated from her mother.

The parting of the daughter from the mother was Katherine's punishment for having a conscience of her own. That Mary was not allowed to visit her even on her death-bed was due to Anne Boleyn's vindictive temper. "The King himself is not ill-natured," the imperial ambassador was to write later, "it is this Anne who has put him in this perverse and wicked temper, and alienates him from his former humanity." Anne's jealousy of Mary was even stronger than her jealousy of Katherine, probably because she could not compete with Henry's affection for his daughter or his pride in her attainments.

Nothing is more characteristic of Katherine than the letters she wrote to Mary after they were parted. She prays God that the amendment in her daughter's health may continue, tries to reconcile her to the loss of the Latin lessons she used to give her by praising the superior qualifications of her tutor, and asks that sometimes she might be comforted by being sent some of her exercises to see. She signs this letter, breathing love through its self-control, "your loving mother, Katherine the Queen." She still signs herself thus two years later when Anne's marriage to the King had been proclaimed and she had been crowned as his queen.

In this letter she tells her daughter to obey the King

her father in everything except in what she knows will offend God. "We never come to the kingdom of God but by troubles." The dictionary definition of religion is "the recognition of supernatural powers and of the duty lying upon man to yield obedience to these". Katherine's religion was the most important thing in her life, and this world was but a discipline to equip her for the next. There was nothing equivocal about her conscience: it was a sharp, shining sword separating right from wrong; there was no overlapping. Her daughter took after her in this respect, but Mary lacked her mother's sweetness and forbearance. Her rigidity was to earn for her a terrible opprobrium from the people and never the love and loyalty they bore her mother.

Henry spent that Christmas at Greenwich Palace, the family home where he had spent it since his childhood days, but now instead of his wife Katherine and his daughter he had Anne at his side. The festivity, glee and excitement of other years were banked against the walls, caught behind doors, the present making echoes of the past. Instead of mirth and merrymaking, there was lavish and sumptuous entertainment of the new French ambassador: Francis had to be courted. If dispute with Rome led to war with Charles, Henry must have as strong an ally as he could find.

In a house that had belonged to someone else, Katherine made Christmas as full of cheer as she could for her small train, and wept in the emptiness of the night to be bereft of Henry's overflowing presence; while their daughter, feeling like an orphan, wondered how anyone could call this Christmas, with no mother to turn to, no father to caress her or give her money to disport herself with and load her with gifts.

At Easter Henry was again at Greenwich, keeping the great services of the Church, always a solace to a man devout but fundamentally irreligious, creeping to the

Cross on Good Friday, sitting among his courtiers on the Sunday listening to the sermon preached by a member of his favourite order, the Observant Friars.

In the chapel bright and glancing with jewel-like colours, rich with ceremonial, the preacher's words, after the divine Hallelujahs, Hosannas and *Te Deums* rising from choirs, suddenly sounded discordant as the knells of a bell. A stir passed over his congregation that did not subside as the stern voice continued to denounce the unlawfulness of the King's proposed new marriage. If he, like Ahab, did evil in the sight of the Lord, then, perhaps, history would record that the dogs licked up his blood as they had done Ahab's.

The following Sunday a royal chaplain was put into the pulpit to plead the King's cause, which he could do with good effect as his sovereign was present. He received short shrift from the warden of Greenwich convent who rose, fierce with anger, and routed him with a battery of blasting words.

The arrest of both malcontent priests did not silence the criticism which was cropping up all over the country, directed by the common people against Nan Bullen. Henry was affronted at such disapprobation: that his subjects should dare to disapprove of what he, their sovereign, approved. Nevertheless his annual hunting expedition into the countries north of the Thames was abandoned, lest it provoke popular demonstrations against the woman who would supplant her former mistress. But opposition always stiffened his determination to have his own way. He was going to marry Anne Boleyn and nothing or no one, Pope, preacher or subject, would stop him.

He raised her to the peerage, the first female peer ever to be thus created. So she was styled Marquis on the charter; he desired her to possess his family title of Pembroke in her own right. It was most unusual, this brief ceremony when the King in the presence of the assembled court slipped over her sloping shoulders the crimson velvet mantle and placed on her bird-like head the coronet. She received a pension of a thousand pounds a year for maintaining her new dignity, and her initials with Henry's, entwined with a true lover's knot, appeared on royal architecture, notably on Wolsey's Cardinal College at Oxford, now known as King's. Katherine was bidden to surrender her jewels for her rival to wear, and Henry left no stone unturned to have her invited to France on his visit that autumn to Francis. Official French recognition would ensure the new Marchioness a cachet in the eyes of the world that Henry was quite unable to bestow.

Francis saw no necessity for a meeting with his fellow king, but Henry, determined to have French acceptance of Anne, was insistent, and good-humouredly Francis gave in, stipulating that everything was to be on the simplest scale and nothing ruinous like the Field of Cloth of Gold twelve years ago.

The problem now facing the French authorities was: which of their ladies was to receive the King of England's travelling companion? Francis's second wife, Queen Eleanor, was obviously out of the question as she was Katherine's niece. Even had she been willing, Henry made it clear he would as soon see the devil as a woman in Spanish dress. He foresaw no difficulty: there was always better cheer without women, and he would be quite content if Francis entertained Madame Anne by himself with great respect; but the French King's good humour did not stretch so far. His sister Marguerite's refusal to play hostess for him left only the Duchess of Vendome available, but because of the scandals associated with her Henry considered her totally unsuitable to welcome his Anne. He was forced to agree that at his meeting with his French counterpart he would be unaccompanied by the newly created Marchioness of Pembroke.

Anne nevertheless travelled with him to France. Henry had not given in yet. The two kings met at Boulogne to conclude an alliance against Charles, and Francis promised to intercede again in Rome on Henry's behalf. The French were realists, and if furthering the King of England's divorce was the price to be paid for winning Henry as an ally against Charles, with his monstrous encircling empire, it was a small one indeed to pay. Henry for his part could not do without Francis in case Charles made war on England. The friendship therefore between the two kings was genuine, as it had not been at the empty charade of the Field of Cloth of Gold.

Francis accompanied Henry back to Calais, where the English King broke the gentleman's agreement on simplicity with a banqueting hall worthy for him to play host to his royal guest. It was hung with silver and gold tissue and decorated with golden wreaths encrusted with stones and jewels. He was attired in russet velvet covered with gold, pearls and precious stones, but the French King beat him at his own game. His doublet was so thickly embedded with diamonds and jewels it had no background to have a colour. Appraising eyes valued it at a hundred thousand crowns (£800,000 in the present day).

After supper eight masked ladies glided into the room to dance with the principal guests. Later Henry himself removed the visors to reveal the beauty they covered, and lo, the King of France found his fair partner was none other than Anne Boleyn whom he remembered as maid of honour to his first queen. Another of the dancers was her sister Mary. Francis rallied successfully, talking to the unmasked Anne for a little time apart, and next morning sent her the present of a costly jewel.

Altogether the visit to France could be counted a success, although Anne had not received the recognition Henry had worked for. But, inveterate gamester that he was, he had other cards up his capacious sleeve that would take more than one trick, and the Joker Fate had slipped him a trump shortly before he left for France. The aged Archbishop of Canterbury, the highest church dignitary in England, died.

Nervous and noisy with bulls ever since the Legates' court, the Pope had inhibited the King of England, under pain of excommunication, from making a second marriage, forbidden the Archbishop of Canterbury to judge the suit, warned the King of England not to cohabit with any woman other than Queen Katherine and, for good measure, prohibited all women to contract marriage with him. Little wonder that Henry found himself with Anne and her faction in the opposite camp, versus the old régime and the *status quo* symbolized by the Pope.

Henry had riposted with act after act passed through an anti-clerical Parliament only too willing to legislate against the clergy, so craven and abject they did not make even the show of a stand. No longer was there a Wolsey to hold the door. The Church in England was stripped of its sanction to make laws except with the King's consent, and was thus stripped of its birthright. The Pope's authority for electing English bishops was abolished; henceforth they were to be licensed by the crown. Rome was no longer to be paid the fees known as Peter-pence when English bishops were consecrated, or like payments: Henry had not yet confirmed this particular act, as it was one of the tricks he kept up his sleeve to be played at a later date. The legislature was tempered by the sanctifying declaration that neither King nor realm meant to deviate from the articles of the Catholic Faith of Christendom. Neither King nor realm had any quarrel with Christendom's Catholic Faith; their quarrel was with the foreigner Pope meddling in their affairs and refusing an annulment. Henry was and remained stoutly orthodox; he was not attracted by Protestant doctrine with its rejection of mass.

139

The old Archbishop of Canterbury had not been a courageous man, but he had been unwilling to judge the King's suit, which was tantamount to declaring the King's marriage to Queen Katherine invalid, when the Pope had forbidden him to do so. Now his office was empty and could be filled by the King's nominee. Henry's choice fell on "a wonderful and grave wise man", who had written a book, founded on Leviticus (the Pope favoured Deuteronomy), proving that the King's marriage was against God's law, and so no Pope could make it lawful by dispensation.

Thomas Cranmer was recalled from abroad where he had been sent to win men over to the King's divorce and when he was taking his first tentative steps towards the new Lutheran teaching. A forty-three-year-old doctor of divinity, he had one of these malleable minds that are coloured and influenced by others, so that, chameleon-like, it changed with his company.

He left England believing what his master believed, that his union to Queen Katherine was against the word of God, and expediently closed his priest's eyes to the knowledge that his patroness, Anne Boleyn, was living in sin with their sovereign. Abroad he came in contact with men who did not view the King of England as the King of England viewed himself. They saw him as a man trying to be rid of a faithful wife that he could marry his concubine. These scholars did not believe in gleaning the Bible for convenient texts to prop up a dubious point of view but searching it for the truth by which the Church could be purged of erroneous doctrine. Under their influence, Cranmer began to blame what his master was doing against Queen Katherine and Princess Mary.

When the summons came from King Henry to return, his ambassador lost no time in starting, but once on the road he delayed his journey. Did he really want to become Archbishop of Canterbury? What about his grave doubts on the propriety of the King's conduct? Did he wish to be associated with another's actions, even if he were king, which he as a priest knew to be wrong? On the other hand, surely it was the duty of a subject to obey and serve his prince. He could not turn now, he had gone too far on the road back. Never would he desert his prince in the middle of a foreign mission. After all, his king was appointing him to the highest position in Church and State. If he held it, he could advance the new Lutheran teaching in England.

"Never man came more unwilling to a bishopric than I did," Cranmer could say. But he came. He was chosen by the King because he and the Boleyn faction felt he would be reliable, i.e. amenable, and they were right. The impress of Henry's forcible mind was to be stamped upon Cranmer's pliant one. If scruples, hesitations or doubts ever troubled the new Archbishop of Canterbury, they did not rise to the surface but wavered and floated in these wan regions of the mind, like fronds of seaweed so pulled and distorted with unseen tides they appear to be what they are not, rootless.

It was vital for Henry that the consecration of his new Archbishop should be recognized by the Pope, essential that the highest Church dignitary in England should have papal authority for his position. For Henry had a great deal for Cranmer to do. Anne was pregnant, and everything must be expedited that the prince to be born was legitimate.

He married Anne so secretly that to this day it is not known where the ceremony took place and who officiated; even Cranmer did not hear of it until a fortnight later. It was towards the end of January, 1533, about St. Paul's Day, probably at Greenwich Palace, by an Augustinian friar well known for his support of the King's cause, that Henry Tudor married Anne Boleyn.

Not a hint of the marriage must get abroad while the

Pope was asked for the necessary bulls recognizing Thomas Cranmer as Archbishop of Canterbury. It was conveyed to his Holiness that if they were not forthcoming Henry would confirm the act forbidding the customary large revenues to be paid to Rome. No longer were English ambassadors allowed to chivvy and harry the Vicar of Christ, they were instructed to "use all gentleness towards him". Two French cardinals made a timely appearance in Rome, asking Clement on behalf of their sovereign to acquiesce over the matter of Henry's bulls. London saw their sovereign arrive in state at the opening of Parliament, and who should have the honour to accompany him on his right hand but the papal nuncio.

Basking in this English sunlight, the Pope was heard to say the King of England was wiser and had a better nature than the King of France. In vain Chapuys, the imperial ambassador in London, who knew everything, sent warning dispatches not to believe the story that the King had given the Lady Anne the marquisate to compensate her for not having received the throne. The coronet had been conferred on her as an earnest of the crown, not by way of compensation. Urgently he wrote that the Pope must be persuaded not on any account to issue bulls unless he made it a condition that Cranmer swore not to interfere in the divorce case. Bitterly he remarked that his Holiness would not be so eager to admit Cranmer as Archbishop if he believed he was a Lutheran.

It all seemed harmless to Clement. He had refused the King of England so much and now this welcome opportunity had arisen when he could do something to please him. With astonishing and uncharacteristic alacrity he issued eleven bulls authorizing Cranmer's consecration, and sent the pall to England.

Henry was saved. Cranmer as papal legate could give judgement that his marriage to Katherine was against the law of God and invalid. He could pronounce that Henry's

142

marriage to Anne was lawful. Never mind if criticism chattered up and down the country about their king marrying another wife before his marriage to his first was invalidated: his rude, ignorant and common people could or would not comprehend that since his marriage to his first was unlawful, he had never been married at all and so was free as any other single man to take a bride.

A bride who was bearing him a son. He was forty-two, in the prime of life, riding the tide when it was full. This was his midsummer, high noontide. His sun was at its zenith, and fulfilment was ripening before his very gaze.

It was Chapuys, the imperial ambassador, who said it. Did the King's Grace really think he would be able to produce more progeny? The Spaniard's voice, soft and sibilant, did not sound as though it were loaded and Henry was off his guard. But his reaction was instantaneous, rebounding before he knew he was struck. Three times he demanded as he blazed with anger, "Am I not a man like other men? Am I not a man like other men? Am I not a man like other men?" The blood that had rushed to his face took long to pale.

CHAPTER THIRTEEN

A KING BEWITCHED

"False luve, and hae ye played me this,
    In the summer, mid the flowers?
I shall repay ye back again,
    In the winter, mid the showers."

HE WAS to remember her when he was old as he had
seen her that day, passing in her litter on her way to her
coronation, her black hair so long and plentiful she appeared to him to be sitting in it. And when he had
anointed and crowned her in Westminster Abbey, he
remembered her joyful smiling face when she said "Amen".
It was a day neither could ever forget, the petty squire's
son who was Archbishop of Canterbury and the merchant's
granddaughter who was now crowned Queen of England.

The citizens of London had lived in their streets these
past few days, crowding to the wharves to watch the
Mayor and aldermen in their scarlet robes bringing *her*
from Greenwich Palace to the Tower, "the King's dearest
wife Queen Anne", with all honour and might, their barges
fluttering with streamers and banners and bristling with
artillery. Music she had all the way, trumpets blowing and

musicians following her in another float and every flag making gay the boats hung with little bells. Everything had been done to amuse and divert the citizens, with a furious dragon on the Lord Mayor's barge twirling its tail, capering for all it was worth and spitting wildfire into the Thames every few minutes.

That was *her* symbol, the white falcon—crowned it was and holding in one claw a sceptre, and that was her motto written large as life, "Me and Mine". You do see what it means, rising out of a tree with a golden stem bearing red and white roses? It means that the red rose of Lancaster and the white rose of York will continue through *her* and her line. "Me and Mine"—the pride of it, and everyone knowing what she is, no better than she ought, no better than any of us. The real Queen would never have chosen such a motto—"Thee and Thine" it would have been with her.

Did you hear what the Bishop of London said?—pity there were not more like him in high places. "The King's Grace, ye say, shall have another wife and she shall bear him a prince. Who hath promised him a prince?" Who has, unless the King himself? If God did not grant a good woman like Queen Katherine one for him, do you suppose He will stoop Himself to her?

The real Queen—it makes a difference, you know, when you're the King of Spain's daughter and not just a Mayor's brat. Did you hear what the real Queen did when they told her she was Prince Arthur's widow and no longer King Henry's wife? She took her pen and drew it through the words Princess-dowager wherever they appeared on the citation. Ay, and she said her name of Queen she would vindicate, challenge, and so call herself until death. "I stick not so for vain glory," said she— true enough, not like some we could name sitting there queening it in her golden dress. "But because I know myself to be the King's true wife"—what we all know, every man-John of us.

King Hal should be ashamed of himself—mebbe, but kings even more than ordinary folk are seldom what they should be. He's no by her, you notice. She's sitting there by her lone self with only her maidens around her. No, he's waiting for her at the Tower. He will no be by her either when they crown her in a day or two. Yon will be *her* day, you see, no his, just like today. No like when he married the real Queen, and they were crowned thegither. Husband and wife *they* were, no King and his—

So much to see, so much to hear, something happening every minute the day before they crowned her, the city's fountains flowing red and white wine for the refreshment of the citizens. She'll pass by this way, her canopy of cloth of gold held over her by four knights. By Fenchurch Street in her golden litter, pausing at the corner of Gracechurch Street, hung with crimson and scarlet, to listen to the speeches of Apollo and his attendants from Mount Parnassus, most cunningly contrived. At Cheapside Cross, all cloth of gold and velvet, wait the aldermen, where the city recorder hands her a thousand marks of gold in a purse which she most thankfully receives. Most gracious she is with her bowings—well, she had the mistress she served all these years to pattern herself on. Mebbe the Mayor and his men are trying to take the bad taste out of the King's mouth when folk at the Easter sermon walked out of a city church before the prayers for *her* could be read.

They have removed the real Queen into the country, to silence and hide her away. They say she stopped one of her gentlewomen from cursing *her*. "Rather pray for her," said she, "for even now is the time fast coming when you shall have reason to pity her, and lament her case." How could that ever be, when they are crowning her the morrow, and every bell in the city is ringing in her honour today?

Here *she* comes by Ludgate, stopping to listen to the choirs singing her praises—her ears will never weary of that. All the scutcheons and angels in Fleet Street have been new painted and, sudden with brightness, appear as though for the occasion. To Westminster Hall, hung with gold arras and newly glazed all because of her, where the King is awaiting her. Such glory and grandeur and triumph will last a lifetime. King Hal can do what he likes but I bare my head to my real Queen and not to her serving-maid, and no cheer will I give as she passes.

The morrow was her coronation day, and Henry watched through a hole in the wall the banquet given in her honour on her return. Earls were her carver, officer and chief butler and her cup-bearer, lords of the realm her lesser servants. That was Wyatt, the poet, who was pouring scented water over her hands. So she sat at table with her ladies—of all the dignitaries only Thomas Cranmer shared her board. Charles Brandon and Will Howard rode into the hall on horseback, escorting the officer and the Knights of the Bath when they entered bearing the first course for the Queen's table, twenty-seven dishes in all. Charles always managed to outshine everyone except Henry, and as Henry was not there his doublet and jacket sewn with orient pearl surpassed everyone else's. How heavy he was growing, his shoulders and back broad as he sat on his courser trapped to the ground with crimson velvet. Mary was not present. Mary was tethered to her manor house in the country. Would she have been there even if she were not ill? Her brother brushed the thought aside; it was of no consequence. The Earl of Sussex, Anne's officer, was kneeling before her with a spice plate so magnificent it took both his hands to hold—what a sweet tooth she had, his little love. Always munching comfets, nibbling at sweetmeats, making a feast of sugar plums.

There were lovers' tiffs even before the crown was secure on her head. Within six months of supplanting her mistress as his wife, Anne, angry with jealousy, was taking him to task for allowing his fancy to rove from her. But the days were past when she had him eating out of her small hand. Roughly he silenced her by saying she must put up with it as her betters had done before her, boasting he could degrade her as easily as he had raised her to the throne.

Her betters? She was his wife and queen, bearing his son. There was no one in the whole wide realm better than she. The law required the presence of the heir presumptive at the birth of the heir apparent. The Princess Mary was sent for, to be in attendance at the birth. Her father was too shrewd to disinherit her yet, lest he lose both Anne and his son in the hazards of childbirth, but when his wife was mother of his heir, then Mary would be degraded from royal rank—Anne would see to that.

The circular to be sent to the nobility announcing the birth of a prince was in readiness. He was to be christened Henry after his father or Edward after his kingly great-grandfather, and Francis had consented to become his sponsor. To think she, Anne Boleyn, was married to one king, had a second as sponsor, and was big with a child who would become a third.

She lay in the old palace at Greenwich waiting her happy hour, in a room where the tapestry on the wall illustrated the parable of the ten wise and the ten foolish virgins. Her long neck looked longer without its collar-band of jewels, and her dark skin was glossed with sweat as she entered travail. The child was not born until between three and four in the afternoon of that Sunday. It was a daughter, not a son.

Henry's disappointment was so great his eyes were sharp

with tears, and Anne needed all her ingenuity to try to soften the blow for him. The circular dispatched to the nobility had an *s* added to the prince to indicate it was female. The child was christened Elizabeth after Henry's mother, and her birth was thought of so little consequence that Chapuys, the imperial ambassador, merely mentioned in his dispatches that the King's concubine had borne a bastard. No premonition warned him that the bastard was to become Queen Elizabeth who would break the power of Spain.

Henry's natural cheerfulness reasserted itself. His new daughter as a healthy child was but the herald of her brothers. He always put a good face on things to Chapuys and in a month or two was telling him he would have a son soon.

Never had he been merrier as he prepared to give such a buffet to the Pope as he never had before. No longer was there any necessity to deal gently with his Holiness, who was now known in England as the Bishop of Rome, all his papal powers having been transferred to the Archbishop of Canterbury. Henry had gone so far without being stopped; he was confident there were no limits to which he could not reach. When he was threatened with excommunication and imperial arms, he snapped his fingers. He would show the princes of the world how small was the real power of the Pope. As for the Spaniards, let them come—perhaps they would not return. He had successfully demonstrated to his subjects, to whom trade came first and foremost, that the Flemish could no more do without their merchandise than the English could do without their custom.

God and his conscience, he informed Chapuys, were on very good terms. He instructed him to tell his master, the Emperor, that the King of England took himself to be right not because so many said so but because he, being learned, knew it. A man, he announced bland with assurance, should rather endure all the censures of the Church than offend his conscience. His conscience was evidently bent on breach with Rome. And the loss of England to the close-knit Holy See was the beginning of the dissolution of the Roman Catholic Church. Impotence to bring its recalcitrant child back into the fold revealed the weaknesses of man-made canon and decree to its enemies, the Reformers, who came storming in with their thunderbolt from God—the Bible.

It has been said by his upholders that Henry VIII liberated the English Church, by his detractors that he enslaved it. In reality he did neither; what he did was substitute himself for the Pope. His subjects looked on in acquiescence, preferring the despotism of their native king to the despotism of a foreign prince of the Church. It must be remembered that their king's despotism did not affect the bulk of his people; it was a minority, chiefly the clergy, who felt its pressure and cutting edge.

The measures before Parliament and Church courts last year were reinforced by Parliament this year. Henry showed England and the world that what he threatened he was strong enough to perform. The English Church still paid the rich revenues they had paid to Rome in the past but now they jingled in their sovereign's pocket, for he was their Supreme Head, the Defender not of papal Faith but of his own. Parliament lopped the clergy's restraining clause "as far as the law of Christ allows", and passed the Act without it.

The Pope, forced to take notice of such defiance, solemnly pronounced sentence in Rome, seven years after the divorce case had first begun, that the marriage between Queen Katherine and the King of England was valid. He might as well not have spoken for all the difference his pronouncement made in England or to its monarch. "You never saw Prince nor man who made greater show of his horns or wore them more lightheartedly," an exasperated

Chapuys exclaimed. He was forever appealing to his master, the Emperor Charles, to declare war on England, although Queen Katherine steadfastly refused to countenance hostilities against her husband or her adopted country.

In Rome bulls depriving Cranmer of his See and excommunicating Henry, Anne and Cranmer were drawn up but not published—yet. With the terrible sentence of greater excommunication dangling over the heads of their sovereign lord and lady, the English court sported, gamed and danced: ". . . Cut off from the Church as long as he lived, removed from the pale of Christian society and deprived of the solace of the rites of religion. When dead to lie without burial, and in hell suffer torment for ever."

That year Pope Clement died, and the Roman citizens forced their way into the room where he lay to stab his dead body again and yet again; they would have dragged his corpse through the streets had they not been prevented. Such savagery was the primitive impulse to destroy what was no longer sacred, to hack to pieces the sacred that had profaned itself.

The King of England's attitude towards the Supreme Head of the Church on earth had undergone cynical metamorphosis since the days he had enlisted himself with boyish ardour as the Pope's knight errant. Since then he had witnessed the Vicar of Christ grant absolution to those guilty of the sack of Rome for the return of his earthly territories. He had seen the men who held the keys of heaven prepared to barter them for unholy gain, to peddle their divine office like so many wares.

Henry VIII, King of England, was a better man than any Pope. Those who wanted proof had only to see how Henry's affairs always prospered because God knew his righteous heart. Let Clement or whoever took his place do what he liked in Rome, he could do what he liked in his own realm. If Paul III declared his predecessor's verdict void then Henry might be prepared to come and go on certain minor details, but he made reconciliation with Rome impossible by announcing his new style to the world, Supreme Head of the English Church, and sending to the block any who denied him the title.

An Act was brought in vesting the succession to the crown on the heirs of the King by Anne Boleyn. None quarrelled with that. Lawyers and clergy alike agreed it was within the rights of Parliament to fix the succession, but it was no longer enough for Henry to know he was in the right to marry again, not enough for the many to say so. Everyone must swear it.

So with the Act went an oath that prominent subjects and all clerics were required to take, swearing first that the King's former marriage was invalid and against the teachings of the Bible. Then, "Ye shall swear to bear faith, troth and obedience only to the King's Grace, and to the heirs of his body by his most dear and entirely beloved lawful wife, Queen Anne."

Now the bulk of Henry's subjects, clerics and laity alike, prominent and humble, were willing to allow, however shocking they considered their sovereign's second marriage, that since he had married again, Anne was Queen and the King's sons by her should succeed to the throne. It was one of these situations that was accepted as a *fait accompli,* no matter how strong the sympathy for the old rejected Queen and her only child. But Henry's nailing Act of Supremacy did not allow the saving grace of acceptance with mental reservations. It left no loophole for individual conscience; the word *only* securely dammed any exit. The King's conscience was to be sufficient for each and every one in his realm. Any who claimed to think for himself was guilty of treason, and worthy of death. Gone were the days when a man could hold high office although Henry knew he did not approve of his divorce, when he could tell his Lord Chancellor to serve God first and after God his king. For the King no longer thought of God and Henry as two separate Beings.

Parliament woke up to the fact, as he began to use them, that they had granted their monarch unlimited powers. He was to be not only king, not only pope, but God to them. Men he had walked with as friends and talked to about the New Learning made the short journey from Tower to block for denying the King's titles.

Sir Thomas More's legal mind could not accept the compromise with his conscience that Cranmer suggested to him, and died saying he was the King's good servant but God's first. The world shuddered at the brutal dispatch of so enlightened and famous a scholar.

John Fisher, with the visionary's far-sighted gaze, he who had spoken out loud and clear for Queen Katherine at the Legates' court, said the King could not possibly take the place of St. Peter's descendant the Pope, their only link with Christ. During his imprisonment Pope Paul, to anger the English sovereign, created him a cardinal; Henry's retort was he would send the new cardinal's head to Rome for the hat. The old man, upright as youth, walked to the block reading the New Testament; his last words were, "This is life eternal to know Thee, the only true God".

And a foreigner wrote home, "In England, death has snatched everyone of worth away, or fear has shrank them up."

Katherine's confessors were burnt alive; they, as members of Henry's favourite order, the Observant Friars, had solemnized and witnessed his first marriage. One, Father John Forrest, wrote from Newgate prison to comfort his queen whom he knew in the gentleness of her heart considered herself the cause of all his miseries: "Would it become, lady mine, an old man to be appalled with childish fear who had seen sixty-four years of life, and

153

forty of these had worn the habit of glorious St. Francis? Weaned from terrestrial things, what is there for me if I have not strength to aspire to those of God?" Priors and vicars who refused to take the corporate oath for their religious houses were hanged, drawn and quartered. Many friars, monks and priests remained "unmoved, unshaken, unseduced, unterrified" after hideous torture for refusing to deny the authority of "the Bishop of Rome" in England.

Their deaths were Henry's defiance flung in the face of the Pope, of Spain and even of France, who had done all she could to effect reconciliation between Rome and England. Christendom trembled at such wickedness and held its breath, waiting for heaven to rain down judgement on its perpetrator. None came. But the constancy of men who refused to deny their conscience was not obliterated by the sickening thud of axe on block, the crackle of flames, or the deaths of prisoners chained to walls: on such sure foundations was the Protestant faith established.

Henry's evil genius was Thomas Cromwell, Wolsey's one-time secretary. It was he who enforced the carrying out of the Act of Supremacy. A man of no scruples, religious or otherwise, he had promised Henry to make him the richest king in Christendom and instilled in him the theory that to be very king his will and pleasure should be regarded as law. Henry preferred to make the laws his will, and had the strength and efficiency to carry his policy out.

Cromwell was now the power at court: the one-time money-lender had become Chancellor of the Exchequer, the merchant made Secretary of State, the soldier promoted to Vicar-General who could recommend bishops and clergy. It was to him one referred if one desired access to the King, he in whose ruthless hands the reins of government resided—for the King. It was to him Queen

Katherine had to write, begging him to tell the King that what she desired above all else was to see her daughter who was ill: "A little comfort and mirth she would take with me, would be a half health to her. For my love let this be done."

Small wonder that Mary was ill; her fate was as unhappy as the stepdaughter in the fairy tale. Present at her half-sister's birth, nothing would induce her to call Lady Pembroke's daughter princess. "Sister," she said, setting her mouth straight, "I will call her, but nothing more." Threats made not the slightest difference to her, and when instructions reached her from her father to change her residence she wrote him trusting that he had not seen the order requiring the lady Mary, the King's daughter, to remove to the place aforesaid, as it left out the name of Princess.

"If I have a son, as I hope shortly, I know what will become of her," said Anne Boleyn. In the meantime Mary's considerable household was broken up and transferred to her half-sister Elizabeth, an establishment which had the magnificence of the rank of which Mary had been deprived. Anne allocated her aunt to be Mary's governess, and told her to box her charge's ears; Mary had to join baby Elizabeth's household where it was Anne's pleasure to make her serve as her half-sister's maid. The only comfort she had was her books, and it was probably the self-control of the girl whose father used to boast never cried that made Anne so vindictive against her. We are jealous of those to whom we feel inferior, and jealousy corrodes the subject, not the object. It says much for Mary's nature that she did not hate the baby who supplanted her but played with her and was amused by the bright little thing's antics.

Henry dare not let mother and daughter come together. He had two fears: one, that there would be a rising on their behalf among his subjects—together that danger was doubled, separate it was halved; the other, that Charles might yet declare war to redress his aunt's wrongs. He knew that Katherine had the power to wage as fierce a war against him as ever her mother Isabella had waged in Spain, but Katherine had no hatred in her except that of being the cause of bloodshed and suffering.

Everyone had to convince him of their loyalty by taking the Oath of Supremacy, and everyone included his first wife and elder daughter. Both refused. Katherine would never swear that Anne Boleyn was queen and Henry's lawful wife. To Catholics she was the King's mistress and her daughter Elizabeth illegitimate.

Suffolk was sent to break up her diminished household, he whom Katherine had shielded from Henry's wrath when he married his sister without permission. Mary, the youngest of them all, was dead now.

And here was Charles Brandon raging in upon her, trying to force her and her servants to take the new oath. Her old Spanish bishop implored her to yield to expediency, but expediency was not in Katherine's vocabulary, either Spanish or English. "We find here the most obstinate woman that may be," Suffolk wrote in his dispatch. Never had woman so faithful servants as she. They stiffly stood in their conscience that she was the Queen and the King's lawful wife. She told them to swear in Spanish the opposite of what the oath said. As she would not go of her own free will, she was forcibly removed in the dead of winter to an inhospitable stronghold with a handful of servants, and the old bishop who was allowed to go as her confessor. He was so timid her enemies considered him harmless, and a confessor she could not be denied.

Mary refused to take an oath dishonouring her mother and declaring herself a bastard. The degree of Henry's megalomania can be gauged when we read that he considered his daughter's refusal the height of ingratitude, just as in the past his feelings had been deeply wounded when her mother refused to temper her principles to the tenderness of his newly awakened conscience.

This inability to countenance anyone's point of view but his own where he personally was concerned can be explained by his upbringing and kingship. He had no sense of proportion, for he had not been schooled as his father had by hardship, deprivation and effort before he climbed the steps to the throne. He did not go softly all the days of his life, remembering the grace of God and a hawthorn tree on a battlefield from which the crown that now rested on his head had been plucked.

His days had been golden all his life with the grace of God which he accepted as his natural climate. The divinity that invested an anointed king clung to reigning monarchs long after Henry VIII's time, and he was robed in it. Not only in his realm but in other lands men praised and asked forgiveness from the crowned head who had sent them to the scaffold. Henry was accustomed to everyone, archbishop and bishop included, prostrating themselves at his feet. He, Sovereign Lord the King, never entered Parliament but he listened to it trusting to his most excellent wisdom, princely goodness, and fervent zeal for the promotions of God, honour and Christian religion, and also in his learning, far exceeding in his Parliament's judgement the learning of all other kings and princes it had read of. It was now second nature for him to believe not only that he could do no wrong but that everything he did was right. He never received a letter from his dearest, from his closest, relative, that did not humbly draw his attention to the unbridgeable difference stretching between him and the writer. But not from Katherine.

He held in his hands the last letter she was ever to send him, for she was on her death-bed.

Between the "My Lord and dear Husband" with which it began and the signature "Katherine, Queen of England", the writer forgave him for the way he had cast her into many calamities and himself into many troubles, and prayed God that He also would pardon him. She commended their daughter Mary to him, beseeching him to be a good father to her. "Lastly, do I vow, that my eyes desire you above all things."

Henry is said to have shed tears when he read her letter; he could overlook the signature now he knew this was the last time she would sign herself thus. He sent the Spaniard Chapuys to her, telling him to hasten and to greet her kindly from him. The ambassador reached her in time, although it was the end of December and the snow had begun to drive in air that clanged with cold.

Anne was pregnant, and all her vitality went into prayers that the child she was bearing be a son. She had not been married for three years yet and had less security with Henry as her husband than ever she had had with him as her lover. The court buzzed with gossip, for there was no privacy, about tiffs and quarrels, coldnesses and umbrage. No longer was Anne the one to hold the cheek, Henry the one to kiss, or rather no longer was Anne the love Henry chose to kiss. It was happening all over again down to the smallest detail: the King's roving fancy alighting on one of the Queen's maids-of-honour, the maid-of-honour squeamish to accept his advances in the initial stages out of reluctance to injure her mistress. But what added to the repetition's nightmare quality was that Anne was no longer the maid-of-honour, she was the mistress.

Henry made so little secret of his preference for the pale insipid Jane Seymour that it was palace common talk. A saying was being bandied amongst midwives, "It is never merry in Enlgand when there are three queens in it." To which one cackling crone rejoined, "There will be fewer soon."

Of course she meant Mary's mother who was ill and

must die some day, put away with all her wits about her in a strong castle in the most inaccessible place that could be found. Anne was the only Queen in England, her predecessor no longer the King's wife or consort. And whoever heard of a lady-in-waiting being called a queen? The child Anne felt leaping in her womb was a son, she was convinced of that; the birth of England's hope would pull the world to rights once more for her and set her where none could assail. That ignorant old crone had probably said "There will be one fewer soon" and the one had been dropped in the repetition.

While she waited for her son to be born, Anne went *devoté,* listening to sermons by a preacher of the new teaching, reading the Bible, distributing alms. She sat amongst her ladies-in-waiting sewing as she used to see her former mistress sit, embroidering a tester for Henry's bed, and helping them to make shirts and other garments for the poor.

The news of Katherine's death followed hard on her last letter to Henry, and the relief at court could be felt. "God be praised," Henry shouted, "we are free from all suspicion of war." Charles had delayed too long to send a punitive army to England; what he had not done to aid his aunt when she was alive, he would not do now she was dead. "Now I am indeed Queen," exulted Anne. They were at Greenwich, and the last of the Christmastide festivities for which Anne up to then had had little heart suddenly bounced with good spirits and cheer.

On the day of Katherine's obsequies—the service to benefit the soul of the departed, often performed by mourners at a distance—the King, his servants and the court attended dressed in mourning as he had commanded. He could wear yellow, the colour of gladness, when he heard of her death, but he had a strong sense of occasion and would not have dreamed of attending the obsequies of his one-time wife unsuitably garbed. Anne, however, dressed not only herself but her ladies-in-waiting in yellow; it was a gesture that cost her dear where her husband was concerned. All her giddy spirits had returned, but she was as jealous of Katherine dead as ever she had been of her living.

Great store was set in these days on how one met one's end. A lifetime could be redeemed by the resigning and repentance of dying, by the shedding of one's baser nature in preparation to meet one's Maker, sorrowing for the wrong one had done and throwing oneself on the mercy of God who alone could deliver, when the naked soul stood on the brink of eternity. And the talk up and down the country was of the good end Queen Katherine had made, of the serenity of a passing that fittingly crowned such a life. In death as in life Anne felt outrivalled by an old demeaned plain woman whose place she could only pretend to fill until she did what her predecessor could not do, present Henry with the gift of a son.

She was brought to bed before her time in the month Katherine died. The premature birth has been attributed by some to the fright Anne received when her husband fell so heavily in the lists he lay unconscious for two hours, by others to her shock when she surprised the mouse-like Jane Seymour sitting on the King's knee. The child she nearly lost her life to deliver was a stillborn son.

Henry upbraided her furiously for the loss of his boy, to which Anne replied with spirit he had only himself to blame, for it had been caused by her distress over his wench.

"Who hath promised the King a prince?" That was what Henry had promised his people when he put aside his first queen to marry his second, and look what had happened. If Katherine of Aragon had not borne him a son who had lived, Anne Boleyn was certainly never going to do so. The signs were unmistakable, God could not have made Himself clearer. He had denied Henry heirs with Katherine because she had first been married to his brother. He was denying Henry heirs with Anne Boleyn because of his former relation with her sister. No good was coming of their union. Henry did not know how he had ever come to marry her in the first place; the only solution to that riddle must be that she had bewitched him. But she could not bewitch God and God had opened his eyes that He refused to bless his second marriage. It would have to be dissolved as his first one had been, the speedier the better.

As always, God and Henry thought the same.

CHAPTER FOURTEEN

"COMMEND ME TO HIS MAJESTY"

> "Oh, Death! rock me asleep,
>   Bring on my quiet rest,
> Let pass my very guiltless ghost
>   Out of my careful breast.
> Ring out the doleful knell,
> Let its sound my death tell—
>   For I must die,
>   There is no remedy,
>   For now I die."
>   —written by Anne Boleyn
>   after her death sentence

NEVER again did the King share bed and board with her. No longer was he Henry to her Anne, no longer were they man and woman together, even husband and wife, but sovereign and his consort who had failed to bear his son alive. When she saw him at all it was in the open gaze of court life. Convention still kept up its play, and when she was strong enough to sit down to dinner, the King's waiter carried to her his Majesty's customary compliment of "Much good may it do you", but never

162

again did he come himself or send for her to share his meal with him.

She who had loved delectable dishes of linnets and rare dotterels had lost her appetite; and even when she regained her health, her spirits flagged. Jane Seymour's absence was now more telling than her presence, and Anne took no part in court life. She spent her time sitting by herself in Greenwich Palace or in the quadrangle withdrawn into her thoughts which, from the expression on her face, were grey. Sometimes she would make a conscious effort to stir herself to play with her collection of little dogs, setting them to fight each other, but these sudden spurts of activity were short lived, and she would revert into inertness once again.

The King had paid in October last year a visit to Wolf Hall, the family home of the Seymours, before Anne had been brought to bed at the end of January and before Katherine had died. It was after that his attentions to the eldest daughter of the house had become marked. Anne knew everything there was to know about Jane Seymour, a characterless creature with nothing to know except that she was the eldest of Sir John Seymour's eight children, so fair she paled into the background, considered the soul of discretion because she, who had no opinion to give, was never heard to voice one.

As Elizabeth had her own establishment at Hatfield, Anne had not her two-year-old infant to divert her, but she never seems to have yearned for her child. The fact that she was a girl when she should have been a boy coloured any maternal feelings she might have, and the only satisfaction she derived from her daughter was the overweening one of placing her above the King's Mary. In all the well-documented accounts of Anne's last days, only once does she refer to Elizabeth and that without tenderness.

Isolated by herself in Greenwich Palace, with her

servants and ladies-in-waiting about her, she was cut off from that other world where wheels were set in motion; from the murmur of voices behind closed doors where a hint became an assumption and eye held eye under lifted brow; from the shuffling between question and answer when they were sorted out, from the little silence after the peroration.

Arrogance did not make for popularity, and Anne had never been popular. Her vituperative tongue had driven her uncle, the Duke of Norfolk, from court when, nerves taut after Elizabeth's birth, she accused him of changing sides and intriguing against her. The accusation was all the more hateful to the Duke because it happened to be true. Others looked upon her as an upstart: but for her usurpation of Katherine of Aragon's place, England would be bound in a profitable alliance to the Emperor Charles instead of to an unpopular one with Francis. And her unwise tongue, the levity of her manners, her familiarity with those who had been her equals before she was queen, and the coquetry of one well armed for the parry and thrust of the duel between male and female, all added grist to her enemies' mill.

"Why are you so sad?" she demanded of Mark Smeaton one spring day when she saw him standing at the round window of her presence chamber. He was of humble origin but so skilful a musician she had elevated him to the office of groom of the chamber.

The reason of Smeaton's loitering at the window was probably to await the opportunity to warn her of what everyone at court but she knew: that William Brereton, friend of both her and the King, had been committed to the Tower after being subjected to examination by a secret committee formed of the Queen's enemies.

Taken off his guard by her question, he replied flurriedly, "It is no matter."

Anne, provocative with boredom and under the impression his pensive demeanour indicated love for her, smartly put him in his place with the rejoinder, "You may not look to have me speak to you as if you were a nobleman, because you are an inferior person."

"No, no, madam," he replied hurriedly, "a look suffices me."

That was on Saturday. On Sunday he was removed to the Tower where he was clamped into iron because, unlike Brereton, he was not of noble birth.

Monday was the first of May, a day celebrated that spring at Greenwich with a more than usual splendid tournament. The King and Queen shared the royal balcony with his close friends. Since his accident earlier that year when his life was miraculously spared, Henry had not jousted, nor was he ever to be able to do so again although he continued to ride and hunt. A spectator now where once he had been the leading exponent, he sat watching the flower of the nobility meet each other in the lists.

Anne's brother, Viscount Rochford, hung up his shield as principal challenger. The Boleyns were a small but close-knit family; they had lost their beautiful and noble mother early, and their father married again, beneath him this time, but their stepmother was always on affectionate terms with her husband's children.

Sir Henry Norris took up the challenge by touching George Boleyn's shield. He was friend of the Queen and so favoured by the King that he was the only person Henry ever permitted to follow him into his bedchamber, and one of the three witnesses of his master's secret wedding to Anne.

The story goes that the Queen, either by accident or design—and knowing Anne it is safe to say it was not by accident—dropped her handkerchief at the feet of Norris who, as any courtier would have done, kissed it when he picked it up.

Instantly Henry rose, his face blackening, and ostentatiously left the balcony, followed by six of his closest friends. He did not speak as he left, and Anne was never to see him again. Uncertainly the joust continued, but the Queen's perturbation was obvious to all, and when shortly she retired, the sports fell apart and broke up.

Versions vary as to when and where the arrests were made but all agree it was within the next couple of days. One report says that as George Boleyn and Henry Norris were leaving the tiltyard they were charged with high treason. At the same time on the same charge Sir Francis Weston was apprehended. Handsome, wealthy and young, he had played cards and dice with Henry and Anne in the past; the King, who unlike Anne was unlucky at games of chance, often lost to him.

Henry rode back to London that day, attended only by six men. One of them was said to be his prisoner, Henry Norris, with whom he rode apart, strenuously recommending him to secure mercy by acknowledging his guilt. Norris repudiated the suggestion that there had been illicit love between him and the Queen, and stoutly maintained his and her innocence. When Westminster was reached, he was sent to the Tower where the Queen's musician, Mark Smeaton, already lay, and whose confession was said to have provided evidence for the several arrests.

In an atmosphere where the very familiar bulked portentous, Anne went through the movements she would have made had everything been normal. As she seated herself at table the following day for the midday meal of dinner, she became aware that something was missing—the King had not sent his waiter to her as always with his compliments. The alarm she felt at this omission was mirrored in the averted faces of her ladies, and she saw some of her servants were crying, tears spurting from their eyes in the manner of their kind. Anne's own foreboding increased until the very air seemed to palpitate with it.

The meal passed in unbroken silence, course following course as though nothing were amiss, beef and mutton taking the place of salad, then fowl and fish, and when they were removed, game. The banquet or dessert was reached at last, all the dishes cleared from the table with the smaller cloth which had kept the larger one clean for the feast of pastries and sweetmeats.

Before they could be served men entered the room, led by her uncle, the Duke of Norfolk. She recognized them all—Cromwell was one, who always seemed to be holding papers in both his short-fingered strong hands— members of the King's council, every one of them, when she came to think of it. As she realized that, she thought, They have come from the King to comfort me for my brother's arrest—he has sent them to reassure me. Then she caught sight of Sir William Kingston. She had seen him only yesterday—only yesterday, a lifetime had dragged itself out since she had noticed Sir William Kingston at the tournament before Henry had left in dudgeon. Everyone had been there and there had been nothing out of the ordinary in his presence yesterday. But what about today? He was not on the council. What was he doing here, entering her presence with these others; what had he come to tell her, the Lieutnant of the Tower?

In terror she rose from her stool and demanded of them all, that she might lose the individual in the crowd, "Why have you come?"

Tersely came the reply, "We have come by the King's command to conduct you to the Tower, there to abide during his Majesty's pleasure."

"If it be his Majesty's pleasure," she replied quietly, "I am ready to obey."

She was put through a gruelling examination by the council before taken to her barge as she had sat at table, without change of habit. Her paramours, her uncle told her, had confessed their guilt. Anne's reaction was instant and passionate, protesting her innocence and imploring to see the King. The contempt in the Duke's replies had the cut of taunts.

She made the same journey from Greenwich Palace that she had made before she was crowned, when she was the King's dearest wife, Queen Anne. People came to the water's edge to wonder as she passed, sitting there by her lone self with men instead of her ladies around her. *He* had been waiting for her at his royal residence then, Henry the husband who used to write her love letters signing himself her servant. What was awaiting her now?

For five centuries the Tower of London had served its kings as citadel, stronghold and castle. Impregnable, it had never been captured, its turrets set with eyes of windows so small they gave it a blind look. From its stout bastions sovereigns had left for their coronation at Westminster Abbey, worshipped in St. John's Chapel embedded in a tower strong enough to last for ever, entrusted the Crown Jewels, kept lions and leopards, and incarcerated their prisoners.

The water slapped against the stone steps as she disembarked at Traitors' Gate and the Tower clock struck five. She could go no further. Slipping to her knees, she cried, "Oh Lord! help me, as I am guiltless of that whereof I am accused." Catching sight of the Lieutenant, who, now she had reached her destination, was prominent, she asked, "Mr. Kingston, do I go into a dungeon?"

"No, madam," he replied, "to your own lodging, where you lay at your coronation."

At that she burst into a paroxysm of weeping which gave way to wild laughter. When she had quietened, she looked about her in a bemused way and said, "Wherefore am I here, Mr. Kingston?"

She asked him to move the King's Highness to allow her to have the sacrament in her closet that she might pray for mercy: what she was asking for was not to communicate, but to have the Host in her oratory for the purposes of adoration. Although described by Roman Catholics as a spleeny Lutheran, she was never Protestant, and clung to the day of her death to the usages and solace of the old religion. She only found herself in the camp of the new reforming sect because Roman Catholics rejected her as the wife of a man who had married her when his first spouse was living, and who looked upon her daughter as a bastard.

"I am the King's true wedded wife," she repeated, denying with vehemence that she had wronged him. To her inquiries about where her "sweet brother" was, the Lieutenant made evasive replies. "I hear say," she said, "that I shall be accused with three men, and I can say no more than—nay. Oh, Norris! you have accused me? You are in the Tower and you and I shall die together. And Mark, you are here too!" She told the Lieutenant that her stepmother would die for sorrow when she heard of her arrest. Her mind flew from thought to thought, never quite alighting until she demanded, "Mr. Kingston, shall I die without justice?"

"The poorest subject of the King has that," the official responded, a reply that drew from Anne a laugh bitter with incredulity.

She asked to be attended by her favourite ladies-in-waiting, but found closeted with her Mrs. Cosyns whom she had never liked and whose position now made her insolent. Worse still, Mrs. Cosyns was accompanied by one of Anne's sworn enemies, her aunt Lady Boleyn. These two women never left her, sleeping at the foot of her bed and greedily reporting statements they said the Queen had made to them in a deposition which was accepted by the council as true. According to it Anne incriminated herself to women she knew to be set over her as spies. "The King knew what he did," she said, "when he put such women about me."

A. F. Pollard, the historian, sums up the case against Anne in his masterly *Henry VIII* thus: "On the other hand, her conduct must have made the charges plausible. Even in these days, when justice to individuals was regarded as dust if weighed in the balance against the real or supposed interests of the State, it is not credible that the juries should have found her accomplices guilty, that twenty-six peers, including her uncle, should have condemned Anne herself, without some colourable justification. If the charges were merely invented to ruin the Queen, one culprit besides herself would have been enough. To assume that Henry sent four needless victims to the block is to accuse him of a lust for superfluous butchery, of which he, in his most bloodthirsty moments, was not capable."

But one culprit besides Anne would never have satisfied Henry; that would have proved nothing to the world and been an insult to him both as man and king. He had to repudiate her as wife and woman, so she could not be made wicked enough, which was why to the accusations against her with three prepossessing accomplices and one low born, incest with her brother was added for good measure. The best that can be said for Henry is he believed what he wanted to believe.

Confession of the Queen's adultery could be wrung from none of the prisoners except from the musician Mark Smeaton and that only after he had been grievously tortured and told if he signed his life would be spared, which promise was not kept. Because he was of low birth, he was hanged, not executed. By his last words at the gallows foot, "Masters, I pray you all to pray for me, for I have deserved the death," he either meant the Queen had committed adultery with him or that he was receiving his desserts for having borne false witness against

170

his mistress. Obviously she expected him to confess her innocence at his end, for when she heard of his death she exclaimed, "Has he not, then, cleared me from the public shame he has done me? Alas, I fear his soul will suffer from his false witness he has borne." The Day of Judgement was not a metaphor in those days but a dread reality; the *e* was still in aweful and it spelt eternity.

When the knightly Norris was offered mercy as the price of confession, he replied he would rather die a thousand deaths than accuse the Queen of what he believed her to be innocent. The four men were tried by a royal commission, and no records of their trials, or of Anne's or her brother's, have been preserved. "If the crown were prosecutor and asserted it," Wolsey once remarked, "juries would be found to bring in a verdict that Abel was the murderer of Cain."

George Boleyn was tried by twenty-six peers chosen by the council from a maximum of fifty-three. He defended himself with such force and point that at first he divided his twenty-six judges. They heard his wife, Lady Rochford, witness against her husband, and listened to the evidence put forward: that one day, when making some request to his sister the Queen, he leant over her bed and kissed her. Yet these men were living in a century when it was the custom for women to hold audiences from their beds, and when kissing was so prevalent in England that foreigners said it was the same as shaking hands among other nationalities.

Kinship would not have stopped the Duke of Norfolk from condemning the niece with whom he had quarrelled; rather the reverse, to prove to the King on whose side he stood. Wherever that massive figure shifted his weight, there would be found Thomas Howard taking up his stance.

There were political as well as marital reasons for the removal of Anne. The death of Katherine dislodged an

171

insurmountable obstacle between Henry and improved relations with Charles and his Empire. Already Cromwell had been told by the Spanish ambassador that though the world—and by the world he meant his master the Emperor—would never recognize Anne as Henry's wife, it might be ready to recognize a new wife.

In the days that followed, as she moved about the rooms she had used when life was at its fullest, Anne's mood alternated between utter despair and hopes dizzy with height. One hour, the Lieutenant noted, she was determined to die, the next the very opposite. She was anxious about her father, and forever asking for her fellow prisoners. Sometimes she could not believe the King intended to harm her. This cruel handling was done to prove her, and at that thought her spirits rose as though she was already saved. "Ballads will be made about me," she said once, adding as an afterthought, "None could do better than Wyatt." He was preserved from sharing the fate of Anne's fellow prisoners, but in a sonnet he was to write later he refers to the danger which once threatened him in the month of May. His sister Mary was Anne's favourite lady-in-waiting who was amongst those brought to the Tower to attend her but, barring Lady Boleyn and Mrs. Cosyns, none was allowed to enter her rooms except in the presence of the Lieutenant and his wife. The notes in the high-pitched score of Anne's imprisonment are flattened occasionally by the comments, bald with common sense, of Lady Kingston, who slept outside the Queen's bedroom. Once Anne predicted there would be no rain in England until she was released, which brought from the Lieutenant the rejoinder, "I pray, then, it will be shortly because of the dry weather."

He was not an unkind man and Anne could have had a harsher warder. Cromwell, the powerful Vicar-General, acted as liaison officer between the King and the Constable of the Tower, and a letter from Anne reached Henry through Cromwell for, four years later, amongst his papers was found a copy marked "To the King, from the lady in the Tower." It was written four days after her arrest, and every aimed sentence reaches its mark as unswervingly as a barbed dart:

Sir,

Your grace's displeasure, and my imprisonment, are things so strange unto me, as what to write, or what to excuse, I am altogether ignorant. Whereas you send unto me (willing me to confess a truth, and so obtain your favour) by such an one whom you know to be mine ancient professed enemy; I no sooner received this message by him, than I rightly conceived your meaning; and if, as you say, Confessing a truth indeed may procure my safety, I shall with all willingness and duty perform your command.

But let not your grace ever imagine that your poor wife will ever be brought to acknowledge a fault, where not so much as a thought thereof preceded. And to speak a truth, never prince had wife more loyal in all duty, and in all true affection, than you have ever found in Anne Boleyn, with which name and place I could willingly have contented myself, if God and your grace's pleasure had been so pleased. Neither did I at any time so far forget myself in my exaltation, or received queenship, but that I always looked for such an alteration as now I find; for the ground of my preferment being on no surer foundation than your grace's fancy, the least alteration, I knew, was fit and sufficient to draw that fancy to some other subject. You have chosen me from a low estate to be your queen and companion far beyond my desert or desire. If then, you found me worthy of such honour, good your grace let not any light fancy, or bad counsel of mine enemies, withdraw your princely favour from me; neither let that stain, that unworthy stain of a disloyal heart, towards your good grace, ever cast so foul a blot on your most dutiful wife, and the infant princess, your daughter; try me, good king, but let me have a lawful trial, and let not my sworn enemies sit as my accusers and judges; yea, let me receive an open trial, for my truth shall fear no open shame; then shall you see, either mine innocency cleared, your suspicion and conscience satisfied, the ignominy and slander of the world stopped, or my guilt openly declared. So that, whatsoever God or you may determine of me, your grace may be freed from an open censure; and mine offence being so lawfully proved, your grace is at liberty, both before God and man, not only to execute worthy punishment on me as an unlawful wife, but to follow your affection already settled on that party, for whose sake I am now as I am, whose name I could some good while since have pointed unto; your grace being not ignorant of my suspicion therein.

But, if you have already determined of me, and that only my death, but an infamous slander must bring you the enjoying of your desired happiness; then I desire of God, that He will pardon your great sin therein, and like-wise mine enemies, the instruments thereof; and that He will not call you to a strict account for your unprincely and cruel usage of me, at His general judgment-seat, where both you and myself must shortly appear, and in whose judgment, I doubt not (whatsoever the world may think of me), mine innocence shall be openly known, and sufficiently cleared.

My last and only request shall be, that myself may only bear the burthen of your grace's displeasure, and that it may not touch the innocent souls of those poor gentlemen, who, as I understand, are like-wise in strait imprisonment for my sake. If ever I have found favour in your sight; if ever the name of Anne Boleyn hath been pleasing in your ears, then let me obtain this quest, and I will so leave to trouble your grace any further, with mine earnest prayers to the Trinity to have your grace in His good keeping, and to direct you in all your actions. From my doleful prison in the Tower, this sixth of May,

Your most loyal and ever faithful wife,
Anne Boleyn

There would be Seymours at court instead of Boleyns. Jane Seymour's face was expressionless as the shell of a crescent moon. Two luminaries could not share Henry's firmament; as Anne waned she would wax, reflecting the golden light of his love.

Ten days after writing her letter, Anne walked into the great hall in the Tower for her trial. An eye-witness records that she presented herself at the bar with the true dignity of a queen. There was not a trace of hysteria in her demeanour as she curtsied to her judges, looking round about them without any sign of fear. The same twenty-six men had sat in judgement on her brother earlier, but he had been removed, condemned, before she was brought in. Standing, she heard the indictment read, after which she held up her hand and stated clearly, "Not guilty", when a chair was provided for her.

She saw the narrow beardless face with its hooked nose and peaked chin of her uncle as he sat in the president's chair; the Lord High Steward of England, he would pronounce sentence. She noticed his son, her cousin, sitting under him as deputy earl marshal, giddy with youth and life and a poet's fancy, all sail had he been a ship, known as the most foolish proud boy in England. And Charles Brandon, Duke of Suffolk—she would receive no mercy from that quarter. The King's illegitimate son, the seventeen-year-old Duke of Richmond, was also one of her jury. He was married to her cousin Mary, daughter of the Duke of Norfolk: strange to think she had brought that marriage about. She had been friendly with her uncle in those days and had so arranged things that he did not need to pay a dowry for his daughter. There was an empty seat where the Earl of Northumberland had sat earlier that morning, but he had been taken ill and had to leave the court. The man who had been Henry Percy in those love-lit days when she had come from France and they had plighted their troth, did not return.

It was reported outside the court that, with her ready wit and eloquence, she, without counsel or adviser, had cleared herself with a most wise and noble speech. Bishop Godwin stated that had the peers given their verdict according to the expectation of the assembly she would have been acquitted, but through the Duke of Suffolk, "one wholly given to the King's humour", they did pronounce her guilty. The Lord Mayor said *he* could not observe anything in the proceedings against her, but they were resolved to make an occasion to get rid of her. As far as can be gathered when all records of the trial have been destroyed, she was condemned on the ground of Smeaton's confession alone, but she was not confronted with him. When she protested that one witness was not enough to convict a person of high treason she was told that in her case it was sufficient.

She heard her doom, to be burnt or beheaded at the King's pleasure, without losing colour, and when she addressed her judges, her words did not falter.

"... I have ever been a faithful wife to the King, though I do not say I have always shown him that humility which his goodness to me and the honour to which he raised me merited. I confess I have had jealous fancies and suspicions of him, which I had not discretion or wisdom enough to conceal at all times. But God knows, and is my witness, that I never sinned against him in any other way. Think not I say this in the hope to prolong my life. God has taught me how to die, and He will strengthen my faith. . . . As for my brother, and these others who are unjustly condemned, I would willingly suffer many deaths to deliver them; but, since I see it so pleases the King, I shall willingly accompany them in death, with this assurance, that I shall lead an endless life with them in peace."

Four days lapsed between her trial and hurried execution. The day before, she took the lieutenant's wife into her presence chamber, locked the door and before six of her ladies-in-waiting told her to sit down in the chair of state. Lady Kingston demurred; it was her duty to stand, not to sit, in her presence, far less upon her, the Queen's, seat of state. But Anne insisted, telling her that title was gone. "Well," said Lady Kingston, "I have often played the fool in my youth, and, to fulfil your command, I will do it once more in my age." No sooner had she seated herself under the cloth of state than Anne fell on her knees before her, imploring her, as she would answer at the Day of Judgement, to kneel thus before her stepdaughter and ask for forgiveness for the wrongs Anne had done her.

The last toll had been exacted, the ultimate clearance imposed. Yesterday she had been taken to the Archbishop of Canterbury, Thomas Cranmer, who had crowned her, sliding down the river to Lambeth Palace in the early morning light, and in a low crypt there heard the primate of England pronounce her three-year-old marriage to the King invalid, thus bastardizing their daughter. Now there was nothing left, and tomorrow could not come swiftly enough for the relief of death.

The King had granted the less cruel death, beheadal, and an executioner was sent for from France, there being none practised enough in England. The hour was not fixed, for the authorities did not want any crowd to witness their victim making a good death, and all strangers were expelled from the Tower.

"Mr. Kingston," she said to the Lieutenant, "I hear I shall not die before noon, and I am very sorry therefor, for I thought to be dead by this time, and past my pain."

"I told her," Kingston wrote to Cromwell, "that the pain should be little, it is so subtle."

At that she put her hands round her throat and said, laughing merrily, "I have heard the executioner is very good, and I have a little neck."

"I have seen men, and women also, executed," the official wrote soberly to Cromwell, "and they have been in great sorrow, but, to my knowledge, this lady has much joy and pleasure in death."

He led her to the block that day, inside the Tower precincts, on the green before the little chapel of St. Peter-in-Chains where the garrison worshipped. She was dressed in a robe of black damask and was said never to have looked more beautiful. One of her attendants was Mary Wyatt, to whom she was seen to whisper something as she knelt. A message she sent to Henry earlier on her execution day no one dared to deliver to him. It was: "Commend me to his Majesty, and tell him he has ever been constant in his career of advancing me. From a private gentlewoman, he made me a marchioness, from a marchioness a queen. And now he has left no higher degree of honour, he gives my innocency the crown of martyrdom."

Legend says she refused to have her eyes covered and that the French executioner, unarmed by the brightness of her eyes, could not do his work with his two-handed sword until, motioning to one of his assistants to attract her attention, he took off his shoes and stole swiftly up to her on the other side.

She had had to remove her coif herself because her ladies-in-waiting were too overcome to help her, but they reverently placed her body in the old elm chest waiting for it that had been used for keeping arrows, and it was hastily thrust away beside her brother in the soldiers' church.

The day before Anne Boleyn was beheaded, it was noticed at matins that the unlit tapers round Queen Katherine's sepulchre kindled with their own light and after *Deo Gratias* quenched themselves. The King, on being advised of this extraordinary occurrence, sent thirty men to witness it. Even from Katherine's tomb, he was receiving confirmation of the righteousness of his acts.

CHAPTER FIFTEEN

TRUMPETS FOR A PRINCE

"My little sweete darling, my comfort and joy,
Singe lully by, lully,
In beauty excelling the princess of Troye,
Singe lully by, lully."

As a dead moth disintegrates at a touch, like the garment
it has eaten, so Henry's memory of Anne Boleyn and all
she had once meant to him was effaced. He wore white
on the day she was beheaded and, when the gun which
was to give the signal she was dead sounded, rode at
once to Wolf Hall. These two facts gave rise to the
persistent legend that he married his third wife either on
the day of his second one's death or the day after. In
reality the wedding took place privately ten days later in
London, and was solemnized by the Archbishop of Canterbury, the pliant Thomas Cranmer, in the Queen's
closet at York Place.

A discerning nobleman noted that the richer Queen
Jane was apparelled the fairer she appeared, whereas the
better Anne Boleyn was dressed the worse she appeared; in
short, Anne's looks did not depend on what she wore and

Jane's did. Jane reaches us in her portraits with the impersonality of a queen on a playing card, for it is the beauty of the clothes she wears that makes the picture, not the wearer.

Anne had chosen as her motto "Me and Mine", Jane's was "Bound to Obey and Serve". It was her passivity and submissiveness that contented Henry after the demanding Anne and lofty-minded Katherine. He was beginning to tire now, and confided to Chapuys that he was growing old, the first time he had made such an admission.

Her docility made her the happiest of his six wives, and would have ensured her remaining so had fate decreed to extend her brief marriage. No party fermented round her in which she was active as yeast, like Anne; neither did her circumstances or personality ever warrant the devoted partisanship that Katherine could claim; but tall handsome brothers received important posts and while she was Queen it was very advantageous to bear the name of Seymour.

She had shown kindness to Henry's daughter Mary before her marriage, and after it did everything she could to reconcile father with daughter. Even taking into consideration that Jane would naturally prefer Katherine's offspring to Anne's, she was drawn to Mary and had understanding how she felt about religion. Henry's wives alternated between following the traditional faith and the new: Katherine had been an unwavering Roman Catholic, Anne favoured the Reformers. Now it was the turn of his third wife to be true to the established. Also, the treatment the girl had received from Jane's predecessor automatically justified the King's marriage with Anne's successor. Jane would have no difficulty in believing the charges brought against her former mistress; she had lived at court until after the Queen's miscarriage, which meant she knew all the scandal, intrigue and titillating gossip of that enclosed inbred world, which would serve to fill in, confirm and heighten the King's picture of his second wife.

The obstacle preventing Henry ever receiving his elder daughter into his presence was the Oath of Supremacy which she steadfastly refused to take. Mary's conscience was very much her own, high principled like her mother's and infallible like her father's. But at the same time as Jane was doing everything in her power to have Mary reinstated at court, pressures were being brought to bear on the girl herself to induce her to conform.

Chapuys visited her some five months after her mother's death in the month of June at the household she shared with her half-sister Elizabeth. The Spaniard believed if anything happened to the King, England would accept Mary as Queen, but if she continued in her obstinacy what had happened to Anne might well happen to her. After all, her lack of submission was dangerous to her father, for she could well supply even inadvertently a rallying point for his potential enemies. So the statesman advised her to obey the King unconditionally; some believe that, present when her mother was dying, he may even have carried a message from Queen Katherine telling her to submit. Advice from such a quarter as the Spanish ambassador, her mother's countryman and confidant, could not fail to carry weight: Mary thanked him for his good counsel and told him she had already written to her father.

Chapuys was Mary's good friend at court. When he returned to London he conveyed to the powers that be his surprise at the heaviness of the Lary Mary's mourning. Hard on his visit came one from the brother of the new Queen, bringing Mary the welcome present of a riding-horse and telling her to send in a list of the clothing she required to the King.

But still no attention was paid to the letters she was sending to her father in the humblest fashion possible, venturing to congratulate him on the comfortable news of his marriage and telling him she prayed God daily to send him a prince, signing herself Your Majesty's most humble and obedient servant, daughter and handmaid.

Cromwell, who had obtained leave for her to write to her father in the first place, sternly exhorted her to do better in her next by telling her the kind of letter she should write.

Poor Mary could not think how to make herself more abject than she had. She suffered all her life from headaches and indigestion, caused by strain acting on a delicate constitution and highly strung, reserved temperament. Now when she forced herself to do what went against the grain, she was nagged with toothache, had a headache that would not lift, and could not sleep. But she wrote out Cromwell's pattern letter word for word—she could not endure to make a copy—and sent it to the Vicar-General to convey to the King.

A deputation from the privy council waited upon her to hear her take the Oath, when Mary promised unconditional submission to all the King required consistent with what she considered the laws of God. But that was not the Oath at all: the Oath was the acknowledgement that her mother's marriage was incestuous and illegal, her own birth illegitimate and the King's supremacy over the Church absolute. The deputation retired circumvented.

Mary received a stinging letter from Cromwell, telling her that her folly would undo her and all who had wished her good. He took God as his witness that she was the most obstinate and obdurate woman that ever was. Unless she signed a book of articles he was enclosing and wrote a letter declaring that she thought in her heart what she signed with her hand, he would make no more effort with the King to effect reconciliation. "If you will not with speed leave off all your sinister counsels, which have brought you to the point of utter undoing without remedy, I take my leave of you for ever . . . for I shall never think otherwise of you than as the most ungrateful person to your dear and benign father."

Mary signed, but that was not enough for Henry. He was taking no chances. She had to repeat her submission in the presence of his council. The only article that was excepted was that which stigmatized her own birth as incestuous.

Her household was re-established, every consideration given to her comfort and she was told she need no longer call Elizabeth princess but sister. As Parliament had made Elizabeth a bastard without declaring Mary legitimate this was not so generous as it sounded, but Mary showed becoming gratitude for permission to address her sister as she had done all along.

That she bore no grudge against the three-year-old Elizabeth is clear in her first letter to her father after her submission. Following its prefatory grovelling paragraph in which she describes herself as his bounden slave, Mary breaks free from Cromwell's tutorage to put in a good word for her demeaned half-sister: "My sister Elizabeth is in good health (thanks to our Lord), and such a child toward, as I doubt not but your Highness shall have cause to rejoice in time coming (as knoweth Almighty God)." And always when the child's name appears in Mary's accounts which she kept herself she is written in as "my Lady Elizabeth's grace".

So Mary's star rose in the ascendant until, through the good offices of Queen Jane, she found herself at court joining in the Christmas festivities at Greenwich Palace. It was nearly seven years since she had lived in the same household with her father but he had always been fond of her, although the impression is received that his pride in his child prodigy was slightly nonplussed when she as a mature woman joined his close circle. In the gay whirl of court life, one quality her contemporaries all ascribe to her and that was virtue.

She was twenty years old now, not unpleasing in appearance, with her father's penetrating small eyes, but tiny and without the attraction that so many small women do possess to captivate and charm. She was an accomplished musician with a swift deft touch and a fine singer, but her speaking voice was discordant and surprisingly strong coming from so little a person. A negotiable asset to her father, she must have been the most betrothed princess in history, but even if she had married, the seal of the spinster was already upon her. It was as an aunt rather than a mother she took charge of her sister Elizabeth at ceremonies, and visited the little brother she was so shortly to have, watching over him with care.

Life was pleasant for Henry in these summer months, showing off his new Queen to the Londoners, gliding down the river with her or joining in the prolonged and elaborate festivities of court life. He was being wooed by both Spain and France who were again at each other's throats. Even the Pope was making friendly advances to facilitate his return to the fold of the Roman Catholic Church, now Anne Boleyn, the bone of contention, was as dead as her predecessor Katherine. But the English King was not thinking of changing his religious policy. He talked with pride of "our Church of England"; the Roman had gone for good.

Monasteries were naturally the most influential centres of papacy in the country, and the lesser religious houses throughout the land were being systematically suppressed and their lands confiscated because of the corruption, slackness and manifest sin Cromwell was claiming to have uncovered in them. The Act was drawn up before his commissioners, called Visitors, returned from their investigations. Cromwell's boast that he would make his sovereign the richest king in Christendom was beginning to come true, for the wealth from the suppressed monasteries found its way by natural course into the coffers of the Supreme Head of the Church of England. Not that these lesser houses were particularly rich; it was the great cathedrals, abbeys and churches that had the wealth—Canterbury for instance with its jewelled shrine of St. Thomas à Becket. But it was comforting to know that the treasury, empty for so long, was beginning to fill.

Superstition too was to be plucked out of the land by its roots and of course everyone knew religious houses were the strongholds of superstition. Pilgrimages were to be suppressed, relics destroyed, saints' days celebrated as holidays abolished (holiday sprang from holy day), and wonder-working images pulled down. In the market-place at Maidstone it was exhibited to the people how the famous Rood of Boxley opened and shut its mouth by an ingenious mechanism and not through a miracle as they had always thought. How these monks had imposed on their fathers who knew no better. . . .

Parliament had brought in these measures, summoned to repeal the Act which vested the succession to the crown on the King's offspring by Anne Boleyn. Members compared their sovereign to Samson for strength and fortitude, Solomon for justice and prudence, and to Absalom for beauty and comeliness. The House was asked to remember the perils and dangers he had suffered and sustained when he contracted his second marriage, and that the Lady Anne and her accomplices had met their due reward. What man of middle life, they were asked, would not after this be deterred from marrying a third time? Yet their most excellent Prince had condescended to contract matrimony again and had, on the humble petition of the nobility, taken to himself a wife whose age and fine form gave promise of issue. Parliament, like God and Henry, thought the same.

186

The new Act entailed the crown on any sons Henry and Jane might have, on any sons Henry might have by a future wife, and on Jane's daughters or any other legitimate daughters Henry might have. The Lords and Commons heartily desired their King's reign to last for ever, but they had to make suitable provision if, when their sovereign went the way of all flesh, he died without heirs. Henry saw to it there was to be no ruinous scramble for his crown after his death. Parliament gave him full authority to give, dispose, appoint, assign, declare and limit the imperial Crown of the realm "to such person or persons as shall please your Highness". It was a unique Act granting unique powers to a unique king. Even from the dead he would pronounce what was to be done by his servant Parliament.

If he had no heir—even his illegitimate son was not spared to him. The boy died of consumption, that scourge that stalked the Tudor race but which by the grace of God had never trailed him, England's sovereign Lord and King. In the meridian of summer at the age of seventeen, Henry Fitzroy, Duke of Richmond, died, whose charm and grace and love of letters reminded everyone of his father. The comely shoot of such a parent tree had been under sentence of death from his physicians for a year. To think that Norfolk's boy, Henry Howard, Earl of Surrey, whom Henry had allowed to be brought up with him, was still alive while he. . . . Only a month or two ago, he had been the first because he was the youngest to pluck his hand from his sleeve and say "Guilty" at Anne Boleyn's trial. A few days later he had watched a queen die on the church green, and shortly before his death had appeared disguised as a Turk at a gay court revel.

Perhaps God never meant to grant Henry a son, but he must not countenance such a thought, only be prepared in case that should happen. He was forty-five, in his middle years but stronger, more active, resolute with health, than a man half his age, than his own son in the flower of his youth. And his third marriage was uncomplicated by these barriers to which God had taken such strong exception in the past.

It came from the north, the rattle of revolt, in autumn, an inconvenient season for warfare. That was where it would come if it came from anywhere. Populous London where he was known was the centre of his popularity; the further he travelled from his capital the less familiar he was to his thinning subjects, and he had never made progress far north. It was unenlightened, clinging to the old faith and a left-off way of living; it had not marched with the times like the south, in step with Henry. He considered his northern subjects rude and ignorant, the most "brute and beastly" of his whole realm.

Not that this rising was against him but against the low-born men in high offices: shear-man Cromwell and tavern-keeper Cranmer, for two. The northerners were demanding their dismissal, the burning of heretical bishops who favoured the Reformation, reconciliation with the Pope, the restoration of the monasteries and the remission of land taxes. It was known as the Pilgrimage of Grace. Thirty thousand men gathered as the army of the Church under a banner displaying the five wounds of Christ. They did not call themselves rebels but pilgrims, and asked to meet their sovereign lord that they could submit their grievances to him personally.

Henry had never heard anything like their presumption, taking upon themselves to amend his laws, as if, after being their king for twenty-eight years, he did not know how to govern his own realm. To pardon or parley with rebels he considered would disdain his honour, but he had no standing army and to treaty was necessary while one was mustered. So Norfolk was dispatched to play for time.

Norfolk was an astute choice. The most unpopular and

difficult undertakings usually fell to him to atone for fore-bears who had fought on the Yorkist side and prove by success his allegiance to the Tudor line. But this commission had a kind of rough justice about it, for Norfolk was of exactly the same opinion as the rebels about the mean men who were his fellow councillors. Henry himself had heard him mutter against the thieves and murderers in high positions. He had snapped back if anyone would not serve as readily under the humblest person he had put in authority as under the greatest duke in the realm; his king would neither consider him a good subject nor allow him to go unpunished. As Norfolk was one of the two dukes in the King's realm, he was suitably crushed into silence.

With skill and vague promises he managed to soothe the leaders, dealing chiefly with one Robert Aske, a lawyer. Their king was a benignant prince and would grant a free pardon to all who had taken up arms if they would disperse. Their demands would be conveyed to and considered by the King himself. Aske must prepare a full statement of them. The King would visit the northern counties, and Parliament would be asked to reconsider the liberties of the Church. On such assurances Aske dispersed his well-disciplined troops while Norfolk in York gathered an army round him.

The lawyer was summoned to London in December to place before the sovereign his statement of the northern-ers' grievances. Henry, affable with good will, lent him the favour of his ear. Their complaints about the Faith were so general they were hard to be answered; the King intended always to live and die in the Faith of Christ. When the Queen was crowned, Henry would like nothing better than for her coronation to take place in York—in spring or summer next year when the roads were passable. Aske returned to Yorkshire secure with promises. All would be well, he told his fellow leaders, if only their monarch's just conditions were obeyed.

But all those who bore the Badge of the Five Wounds were not single-minded pilgrims; many were men with political and economic scores to settle. When these extremists saw no signs of the government fulfilling their promises, they broke the truce. This was the chance and now was the hour to recall the free pardon.

Henry examined the evidence sent to him against the plotters like a "detective policeman". Norfolk was instructed to cause dreadful execution upon every town, village and hamlet that had offended in this rebellion; all the leaders, including the innocent Aske, were executed. Instead of a Queen's coronation in the white city of York, courts were set up that spring and summer throughout the northern counties. Even those who had laid down their arms and fulfilled the royal obligations were not spared, and Norfolk was told to show no pity to abbots and monks who had joined the Pilgrimage. Once and for all Henry would stamp out revolt in his realm and make rebels a terrible example to the rest of his subjects.

That January was so severe the Thames froze. It was remembered because the King and Queen, attended by their entire court, crossed it on horseback to Greenwich Palace. London learnt the Queen was with child when a service of thanksgiving was held.

Henry did not move about much that spring because his leg was troubling him again. This was a varicose ulcer in his thigh, called in contemporary accounts "the King's sore leg". It was described that year as somewhat sore, which was an understatement for the condition was now chronic, the patient never giving it a chance to heal, and this spring both legs were affected.

No longer did he hunt as in the old days, pursuing the chase with his hounds, but shot from a stand or butt. Riding must have been acutely painful because of his leg, but his subjects were unaware of that as they watched him pass on long progresses, visiting his ports and harbours, inspecting defences—more peremptory in his look perhaps but still benignant towards them, a little bigger each time he passed their way. For he was fast putting on weight. Unable to take the excessive exercise of earlier years, to join in the athletic pursuits in which he had no rival, he continued to eat enormously.

He remained near his consort while she was carrying his child, lest she should hear any sudden or unpleasant rumours blown about if he were absent from her. After all she was but a woman, and women were prone to idle fancies. He was remembering Anne's miscarriage which some believed was caused by the shock she sustained being told of his accident when he was thought to be dead, but which Anne herself attributed to her distress over his penchant for Jane Seymour.

His additions to Wolsey's rose-red Hampton Court were finished now, the splendid banqueting hall completed, a tiltyard added, butts for archery, bowling alleys and, for his favourite game, a tennis court—a prince of the Church's palace made into a country residence for an athletic king. The Queen's lodgings begun for Anne, whom he had brought here after her coronation at Westminster Abbey, were completed and, because London was sick with a visitation of the plague, were used for Jane's lying in. Her initials took the place of Anne's twined with his; in some of the true lovers' knots the J for Jane does not quite cover the superseded A. Henry's arms on the right of the chapel entrance faced Jane's on the left: the unicorn, with a collar of roses round its neck, was adopted for her as the emblem of chastity.

Her labour was a martyrdom of suffering; she endured thirty hours of travail. The story of the King's reply, "The child by all means, for other wives can easily be found," when asked whether his wife or child was to be spared can be discounted. No medical man or attendant would have dreamed of putting such a question; it went without saying that the child at all costs must be saved, to which the mother would have been the first to accede.

Jane gave to her husband the crown of his life, a son and heir. There were no doubts about whether he should be called Henry or Edward: arriving on the vigil of St. Edward, 12th October, 1537, the child decided for himself it was to be Edward.

The noise of that age was deafening and it was like an accompaniment to the King himself. Even when he went to a masque he was attended by sixteen torchbearers and the rat-tat of drums, and guns shot off at his landing for an evening's entertainment would rumble in the air like thunder.

Exaltation at the Prince's birth exploded into bell-ringing, gun-firing, singing, cheering, feasting, and music noisy with triumph and joy. Hampton Court rang, and the goodly sound of the trumpets at his christening was remarked upon for its loudness.

It took place three days after his birth and at night. The mother, wrapped in crimson velvet furred with ermine, was moved for the occasion from her bed to a pallet sewn in gold thread with the crown and arms of England. From this she handed her baby over to be baptized. At her side sat the King, and he remained there throughout the hours-long christening, and was not present as custom guided at the ceremony itself in the chapel.

It was midnight when they heard the trumpet flourishes at the entrance of the silver-stick gallery announcing the return of the procession. The Prince had been baptized by the Archbishop of Canterbury and proclaimed by Garter King-of-Arms: "God in His Almighty and Infinite Grace, grant good life and long to the most high, right excellent, and noble Prince Edward, Duke of Cornwall and Earl of

Chester, most dear and entirely beloved son of our most dread and gracious lord Henry VIII."

They brought him in, their christened son, with trumpet notes, under a canopy of state, to hand him to his mother that she might be the first to call him by his Christian name. Nothing could ever take that moment from Jane Seymour. For all time she was rooted in the family tree of England's history.

Nothing would ever take that moment from Henry as he saw his own likeness in the face of his son, bone of his bone, flesh of his flesh, lying big-browed amongst the cushions with his little star-fish hands.

CHAPTER SIXTEEN

ROSE WITHOUT A THORN

" 'Ten thousand times I'll kiss your face,
And sport, and make you merry.' "

THE Queen took so ill the day after the christening tha
all the rites of the Roman Catholic Church were ad
ministered to her, but rallied sufficiently to raise hopes o
her recovery. The betterment, however, proved to be th
delusive pause that so often precedes death and she die
between sunset and sunrise twelve days after the birt
of her child.

Henry sent an exulting letter to Francis on the birt
of his son: now his rival had no advantage over hin
Even the death of the mother could not diminish th
exaltation for a prince of the Tudor line, although b
felt the loss of his wife keenly. "Divine Providence," b
wrote to Francis, "has mingled my joy with the bitterne
of the death of her who brought me this happiness."

He took his bereavement heavily. He did not want
be spoken to and left Hampton Court as soon as he coul
withdrawing into himself. His council saw to the funer
arrangements, and his daughter Mary as chief mourn

kept nightly watch with the dead Queen's ladies around the embalmed body. The obsequies lasted for three weeks on the orders of the King: daily services, nightly vigils, tapers burning on the altar night and day; the chapel close round the treasure of its dead, the air heavy with incense; the stumble of the unuttered prayers of the mourners, over-hung with a suspension that grew unbearable until some movement, such as the black-robed figures replaced by others, shifted the momentum which began to mount imperceptibly again.

Jane was Henry's only wife for whom he wore mourning. He hated black or anything that reminded him of death, and there was a scene should someone inadvertently come into his presence in the sable clothes that betokened loss. But for Jane his wife, the mother of his son, he wore mourning throughout Christmastide like his court, and did not change till Candlemas.

His genuine sorrow for his wife's death did not stop him taking preliminary political steps for providing himself with a new queen. He could make a French alliance which would annoy Charles and strengthen his friendship with Francis, or he could choose an Empire bride which would annoy Francis and strengthen his friendship with Charles. The surprising thing was neither Charles nor Francis appeared to set much store on gaining England's king as a marriage asset. Indeed the two rival kings were showing regrettable but unmistakable signs of wishing to terminate their mutual warfare which was draining their resources and benefiting only England. For, locked in hostilities with each other, neither could take advantage of Henry's vulnerability when his northern subjects rose in revolt.

Henry began hopefully enough by suggesting to Francis's ambassador that Frenchwomen suitable by birth and their good looks for his bride should be sent to Calais where he could inspect them in person, and get to know them some time before deciding. "I trust no one but myself," he told Marillac; "the thing touches me too near." The sardonic Marillac's reply in his native tongue about testing the ladies' charms sent the Englishman's colour flaming to his face.

He asked for the hand of the very tall young widow who had been born Marie of Guise, although she was already engaged to his nephew, the young King of Scots. But Henry had not the slightest doubt that when he appeared on the scene the promise to James would be broken and at the same time the traditional "auld alliance" between Scotland and France. Jovially he said he was big and needed a big wife. James, however, sitting so conveniently on his uncle's doorstep, was far too important an ally for Francis to offend. Henry was offered instead the plain, sickly princess his nephew had already rejected, which he could not be expected to take in good part.

The well-known story of the royal duchess who said that if she had two heads, one of them would be at King Henry's disposal, has been attributed to both Marie of Guise and Christina of Denmark. Christina came under her uncle, the Emperor's sphere of influence; she also was very tall and a widow although only sixteen. The English King commissioned his court artist to paint the portraits of potential brides and Holbein executed Christina's in a three hours' sitting at Brussels. Henry's courtship of her went on for the best part of two years, blowing hot and cold as the political scene dictated, although he accused Charles of "knitting one delay to the tail of another", and instructed his envoys to assure Christina how earnestly "we have been minded to honour her with our marriage".

Cromwell was now ready to bring the greater monasteries into line with the lesser by suppressing them. They had escaped earlier because although his Visitors had revealed the smaller ones as dens of iniquity it was considered religion in the large solemn ones was right well

196

kept and observed—for the time being. The hour was now ripe for them to receive visitation.

That there was slackness in religious houses is undeniable, and grave abuses in many. An Order does tend to grow laxer, never stricter, as time intervenes between it and its founder's pristine simple Rule. Throughout Henry's reign isolated bishops drew attention to monastic reclaim; they had discovered disorder in one, enormities in another. It was Wolsey's glorious opportunity to effect reformation but his hands were too occupied with statecraft, his eye too trained on the papal throne and its next occupant, to do more than write out detailed instructions for the improvement of monastic devotions.

Indeed he had been the first to suppress some twenty-three monasteries and three nunneries, putting the proceeds towards educational endowments dear to his heart, and many considered his fall was God's punishment for such robbery. True, each community he suppressed had dwindled to fewer than twelve surviving inmates but they had grown into their neighbourhood and their ejection was fiercely resented. The citizens were not appeased when told it was better to have forty of their children educated and afterwards sent to Oxford than to have six or seven canons living amongst them. Indeed at one place they turned out the agents Wolsey employed to enforce his instructions, reinstated the canons and told them if they were again molested, to ring their big bell, when they would have immediate assistance.

The Cardinal's two agents had been hated as they rode about the countryside from one religious house to another carrying out their master's orders and accepting large bribes to exempt certain communities. One rode accompanied by a train of hangers-on, as though he were making a royal progress. The other was Thomas Cromwell.

His programme for the dissolution of the large monasteries worked out ahead of schedule. The measures against these religious houses that had joined in the Pilgrimage of Grace had taken all the heart out of brother- and sisterhoods throughout the country; only a dozen out of hundreds had to be threatened into submission. Better to accept the pensions they were offered than lose them in an unavailing fight. The world had turned upside down and there was no place in it for them now the splendour, wealth, authority and power of the old faith was being gripped by the crown. The ecclesiastical splendour, authority and power had themselves superseded the ancient Rule of poverty, chastity, obedience, which gave the founders that grandeur of the spirit that asked only for the essentials.

But it was not only nuns, monks and friars who were turned out of nunnery, convent and monastery. Every foundation had its own household, a community in itself, its servants and tradesmen not in holy orders, who found themselves without livelihood and home when the parent house was destroyed. And there were the skilled craftsmen, the makers of vestments, robes and copes, of altar cloths and wax tapers, crosses and crucifixes, beads, reliquaries and images, whose markets disappeared when shrines were rifled and altars plundered.

It took twenty carts to carry away the treasure of St. Thomas's shrine in Canterbury, England's mother church. The finest jewel in Europe, a French King's offering to St. Thomas four centuries ago, was made into a ring for Henry's big thumb. "A cloister without books," wrote St. Benedict, "is a fort without an armoury." Centuries of library-arsenals were destroyed at the dissolution of the monasteries, priceless illuminated manuscripts thrown out as though they were rubbish after being torn from their jewelled covers. And no one cared, not Henry, the patron of the arts, the enlightened lover of learning, in their greedy haste to get their hands on the Church's buildings, lands, wealth and possessions.

198

It was the monasteries who provided hospitals for the sick poor. London was full of them: St. Bartholomew's, St. Thomas's, St. Mary Spital, Elsing Spital for the blind, St. Mary of Bethlehem (Bethlem, Bedlam) for the insane, the House of St. Augustine Papey for old priests. All disappeared. The city authorities wrote to the King about the great infection and other inconveniences this had caused, but Henry paid no notice until he needed money and credit from the city. Then he refounded St. Bartholomew's, only to take it back when he received what he wanted. His physicians, a band of wise and upright men, said the only way of getting the King to listen to reason was to have him fall ill.

The citizens of London went about their business as though unaware that no longer cowled monks in black, white or brown habits with rope girdles were to be seen. Only their own numbers were swollen disproportionately with an influx of vagabonds, rascals, masterless men and the wretched poor who were always with them, while their city fell suddenly and strangely silent without the chiming, ringing and pealing of cascades of bells.

No more processions to watch as abbot or friar went by in a forest of crosses and sconces and standards, or pause as the relics of the saint were borne past. There were no relics now: the Blood had been found not to be blood at all; the splinters of wood not from the Cross; the saint's shoe replaced when it wore out. It was still the people's duty to go to church on Sunday morning, to attend the services at Easter, Christmas, Trinity and Whit. Holidays might be abolished, but not fast days.

The King had commanded out of the goodness of his heart that a copy of the Bible should be placed in every church and that the priest should read from it to the people in their own tongue, that they might learn the Word of God. He was to recite the Lord's Prayer, the Creed and the Ten Commandments in English that his flock could learn them by degrees, and before anyone could receive the sacrament at the altar he must satisfy his shepherd he knew the rudiments of the faith.

The Lutherans saw in the dissolution of the monasteries the dawn of the Reformation breaking over England, but Henry's principal Protestant leaning was that towards the Bible which was to him "that most precious jewel, the Word of God". He hated Lutheranism, and upheld the doctrine of transubstantiation, celibacy of the clergy and the traditional liturgy of the Church.

The Reformers did not think of their, the Protestant, faith as new. It was called thus only to distinguish it from that of the Roman Catholic, for they did not abolish an old church to establish a new one in its stead. To them reform meant re-form, to make better by removing, or become better by abandoning, imperfections, innovations and faults. They claimed to re-form the Church of Christ in terms of the age of His first apostles. Gospel truth led them not to Rome but to where One sat with His disciples in a bare upper room. They replaced the infallibility of a Church with the infallibility of the Bible, and they freed the Lord's Supper from the elaboration, symbolism and ritual of the Mass.

Like most of his subjects Henry was orthodox to the core, and why he carried them with him in what he chose to do was because of this identification between them. He had that inestimable gift as a leader: he knew when to stop. Not only the Pilgrimage of Grace warned him not to go too far or he would alienate his subjects but his inclination.

Their giant of a King hung with jewels, in his ruby collar and his coat of cloth of gold buttoned with diamonds and rubies and sapphires, this great father figure more than life size like the embodiment of England, a transcendent prototype of the common man, personified both the best and the worst of his people.

If Henry's actions against the old faith heartened the Reformers, they shocked and horrified Rome, and dismayed his one-time allies Charles and Francis. Pope, King and Emperor all met at Nice where Paul negotiated a ten years' true between the two rulers. In this atmosphere of fervent friendship, the long-cherished project of a joint attack on the outsider England was considered. The Pope as his contribution took upon himself to encourage Scotland to invade her neighbour at the appropriate time. Henry was isolated, without an ally.

Cromwell was more apprehensive of the situation than his sovereign. Henry at once set about seeing that the defences along the coasts and on the Scottish border were repaired and strengthened. The ulcer on his leg suddenly clogged that spring so that for ten to twelve days he was dangerously ill, black in the face, unable to speak, his breath stifled. But that did not deter him travelling a month or two later to inspect in person the fortifications he for years had been erecting at Dover at great cost. Everywhere his subjects surged forward to help, lining their shores with palisades, repairing beacons, digging dykes and throwing up ramparts. Even women and children worked with shovels at trenches and bulwarks. Let them come, Scot, Spaniard, Frenchie—England was ready for them, England and her King, her King who was England.

Cromwell was not a religious man but his politics inclined him towards the radical Reformers and away from the reactionary old faith. For some time he had advocated an alliance between England and the strong Protestant princes in Germany who were as much a thorn in Charles's side as his neighbour Scots were to Henry. Such a bloc of united interests would seriously threaten the Emperor's hold on his Dutch dominions, so vital to English trade. But Henry had been lukewarm because of his distaste for the uncompromising Lutheranism of his proposed allies. Only when Charles began to accumulate guns and ammunition in the Antwerp area, preparatory to invasion of England, was he prevailed upon to form a precautionary alliance with them and Denmark.

To make his plan doubly secure Cromwell was pushing for all he was worth the marriage nostrum which, despite the lessons of the past, was still believed to act as cement binding nation to nation in indissoluble union. Who more suitable for a bride for the King of England than a member of the House of Cleves? With his family claims to the Duchy of Guelders, the Duke of Cleves was the very barb of the thorn in Charles's side, his lands most favourably placed for invasion of Charles's dominions should the need arise. And he had sisters for the picking.

Holbein was dispatched to paint the portraits of the two sisters Anne and Amelie; Anne was chosen. Henry, and posterity, considered his court artist excellent at making likenesses but he has been accused on this occasion of flattering his subject. So delectable did he portray her that the legend arose he fell in love with his sitter, a fellow German, as he was painting her. Even a plain woman has her moments, and Anne's moment may well have chimed with Holbein's hour.

Her very age might have given Henry's advisers pause: she was thirty-four, old in those days for a woman. And the pen of Henry's ambassador did not run away with him, whatever happened to Holbein's brush. His description is a decided monotint. "The said lady" occupied her time with her needle; her virtues of gentleness, sobriety and gravity which he mentions are all estimable but unsprightly. She could read and write her own language. There her attainments began and ended for she knew no other, nor could she sing or play any instrument. The ambassador took some pains to point out the Germans considered it unseemly for their great ladies to be learned, and music a frivolous pastime. He was of the opinion she would soon learn English once she put her mind to it, but he obviously could not picture the said lady disporting herself at Henry's sophisticated court. He inferred her brother, the Duke of Cleves, was serious enough but lively compared to his sister Anne.

It was Cromwell who assured his King that everyone praised the beauty of Anne of Cleves, both of face and body, and that she excelled the lovely Christina as the golden sun did the silver moon.

The marriage treaty was concluded and Henry had the satisfaction of the man who discovers on doing his duty he is pleasing no one so much as himself. He agreed to forego a dowry since his brother-in-law was in financial straits. For two years he had been wifeless and was agog to meet his bride.

She travelled towards the end of the year and was stormbound at Calais for well over a fortnight, which meant she had to spend Christmas on her journey instead of with her bridegroom. But she was received with all pomp in the port town, and admired the King's ships *Lyon* and *Sweepstakes* until they let off a hundred and fifty rounds in her honour which caused so much smoke none of her lengthy train could see any of the others. The time waiting for a prosperous wind was spent pleasantly enough with the English lord admiral trying to teach her cards, a very necessary accomplishment for the bride of the gamester King of England.

Henry, on the other side of the Channel, could hardly restrain his impatience. When he heard she had disembarked at Deal, he determined he had waited long enough. It would be days before her train reached London on winter roads for her state entry. He told Cromwell that he sore desired to see her grace and intended to visit her secretly next day, "to nourish love".

Accompanied by eight lords-in-waiting, all dressed the same as he was, travelling incognito, he posted to

203

Rochester where his bride-to-be was resting to present her with his New Year's gifts in person. Boyish with eagerness, he entered her presence.

The interview is said to have lasted only a few minutes, and scarcely twenty words were exchanged. Anne's German was guttural high Dutch, and German was not one of Henry's five languages. Henry withdrew almost at once. An eye-witness testified that he had never seen his Highness so marvellously astonished and abashed. It is the one occasion on record that Henry was at a loss for words.

He found his voice when he sent for his lord admiral and demanded, "How like you this woman? Do you think her so personable, fair and beautiful as she has been reported to me?" Cleverly the sailor evaded a direct reply by remarking he would call her complexion brown, not fair; and he would have none of it when Cromwell tried to shift the responsibility on to his shoulders. So he should have detained her at Calais, should he, and told his sovereign she was not as handsome as she had been reported? But he had been invested with no such authority; his commission was to bring her to England, which he had done.

"If it were not that she is come so far into my realm," Henry declared, "and the great preparations that my state and people have made for her, and for fear of making a ruffle in the world, and of driving her brother into the hands of the Emperor and the French King, I would not now marry her."

There was no remedy. He had to put his neck into the yoke and wed what he called a Flanders mare.

Someone would have to pay for this. His head was not too much to ask for placing his sovereign before the whole world in so humiliating a position, making him a laughing-stock. Cromwell had no friends: he was too successful, too rich, too ruthless to have accumulated goodwill as he battled to power. Now his enemies gathered round the cockpit to glory in watching the conqueror, all spurs and crop, conquered at last.

They had to wait a month or two. When it was rumoured abroad he was tottering, Henry raised him to Earl of Essex. The King's small mouth pinched itself even smaller as his face stoutened round it, his watchful small eyes withdrew even further, like a mole's that are buried in its fur to protect it from the dust and grit it throws up.

The wedding took place almost at once. Both the French and Empire ambassadors had been invited to witness a ceremony that was to have been a diplomatic and personal spectacle of triumph. No expense had been spared, with the coffers bursting with monastery gold. Marillac noted that five thousand horsemen rode in the procession.

Henry put on as gallant a face as he could; lovingly embracing and kissing his bride in public. He was dressed magnificently in a crimson satin coat slashed and embroidered, his cloth of gold doublet raised with large silver flowers and richly furred. His Queen's costume was every bit as costly, thickly embroidered with pearls, but it was made in the unbecoming Dutch fashion without a train. Her jewelled crown sat on a wig of long luxuriant yellow hair. Marillac described her as "tall of stature, pitted with the smallpox, and has little beauty. Her countenance is firm and determined."

Henry had the endearing habit of calling all his wives Sweetheart, and he addressed Anne thus when they were together. In public he treated her with the courtesy due to his Queen. But he averred from the first he would never have a child by her, and his distaste of the whole situation grew more and more pronounced until he had not the palate to continue it. He was accustomed to the society of cultured women: Katherine had been his intellectual equal, Mary and Anne Boleyn had both been educated in France, and Anne's vitality made her like an arrow that was always travelling. This woman's phlegm was not Jane's docility: she was not submissive, she was stubborn, and the clatter of her ugly tongue was an affliction to his musical ears. They had no common ground on which to meet.

That she found sharing the King of England's bed as unpleasant an experience as he found it with her can be judged from her reply when some English court ladies tried to inveigle her into saying that the King had neglected her. She denied he had done any such thing, affirming she had received quite as much of his Majesty's attention as she wished.

Perhaps the best testament of Anne of Cleves is contained in the few words of the English historian who wrote, "Well, it pleased his Highness to mislike her grace, but to me she always appeared a brave lady."

Marillac ran his practised eye over her German ladies-in-waiting and pronounced them even inferior in looks to their mistress, their dress so tasteless that a beauty would have looked a fright. Anne had hoped to keep them beside her as companions in a foreign country, but it was made clear her household must be English.

There had been a scramble for the coveted appointments of lady-in-waiting amongst young Englishwomen before her arrival, strings pulled, influence brought to bear, presents of Gascon wine and barrels of herring placed in the right quarter. The maids of honour to Queen Jane had an advantage over newcomers. Having access to the King, they could make offerings of quince marmalade and damson cheese, writing to their mothers in high glee to send more as soon as could be, so acceptable were they proving.

Young Katherine Howard had not been one of Queen Jane's attendants and she had no mother to press her suit for her. Nevertheless she won her heart's desire, an appointment at court, because she was niece of the great Duke of Norfolk.

She had red hair and was always laughing, her dimples snug in her pretty cheeks, a young girl but so diminutive she could have been taken for a child. No one would have guessed looking at her that she was so experienced a child. Her aunt had warned her she would spoil her beauty if she were not careful, but her beauty was not spoiled. She knew how to look after herself.

All these days were behind her now, she was as maidenly as any of her court companions. Life was quite different from what it had been when she had been sent to her stepgrandmother, the redoubtable Dowager Duchess Agnes, to learn all housewifely arts, sharing the long dormitory with her grandmother's highly-born attendants and their servants. But learning how to govern and direct house and kitchen, embroider and play the virginals, did not occupy all Katherine's time in the Norfolk country mansion at Lambeth, embowered in orchards and gardens that ran to the very edge of the Thames. Not when her music master was Henry Manox. They used to meet in the little room the Duchess used behind the chapel. How fond he had been of her, how very fond, suing her to give him a token of her love. She had soon put him right there— as though a low-born music teacher could expect a token from her with Plantagenet blood in her veins.

But blue blood did not mean wealth. Her soldier father, whose valour and military skill had been largely responsible for the Flodden victory, had never been rewarded and was penurious. Katherine had ached for silks, satins and velvets.

Dereham, her young kinsman, used to give her things: sarcenet to make a little quilted cap, a fine Holland shirt embroidered with point and needlework to make into articles for her wardrobe, a silk pansy and another artificial flower called a French fennel they said all the ladies at court were wearing—before she dare wear that, she had to prevail on indulgent Lady Brereton to say she had given it to her.

Dereham belonged to what her uncle called his household troop, all gentlemen and most kin to him, whom he kept handy to be ready in times of strife or neighbourly quarrels. Dereham and other young gallants used to steal up to the long dormitory for midnight feasts, bearing with them delicacies left over from the banqueting table in the great hall below—wine, strawberries, apples and other rare things to make good cheer. There was a convenient little gallery where the young men could hide should a suspicious Duchess Agnes happen to pay a reconnoitring visit.

They had exchanged love tokens, she and Dereham, and he had called her wife. How they had kissed, clinging to each other with their lips like two sparrows. Her grandmother had surprised them once and had boxed Katherine's ears, asking them if they took her home for the King's court.

When it was discovered there had been more than kissing, Katherine was beaten and her lover fled. Their stolen farewell had been tempestuous with grief, and Katherine had employed one Jane Acworth, a readier writer than herself, to carry on a secret correspondence with him for a time.

She did not know where he had gone; some said it was out of the country, and now she did not care. She was well quit of him with his possessiveness. Manox, Dereham and the ready writer, the nurse Mary Lassells who had slept in the dormitory—every single one of them had been swept clean out of her mind. The present was sufficient for her, the scintillating irresistible present—maid-of-honour to the Queen, at the King's court full of gentlemen-in-waiting, gentlemen of the privy chamber, gentlemen this and gentlemen that, and the handsomest of them all, her cousin Thomas Culpeper. The very mention of his name had made Dereham blacken with jealousy.

She was in the brush and stir of court life, heard all the gossip going its rounds. Do you know what his Majesty said when he heard the Princess Elizabeth ardently desired to see the new Queen? "Tell her," he said, "that she had a mother so different from this woman, that she ought not to wish to see her." That was the first time he had even been heard to mention Anne Boleyn since . . . She of course was Katherine's cousin, which made little Elizabeth her niece.

Her uncle the Duke had newly returned from France where he had been taking soundings. He told his sovereign the French King was not likely to join in any alliance against England. It was Cromwell and his ecclesiastical policy of which Francis disapproved, not Norfolk's king.

Everyone had known, when the Emperor dispersed his fleet last year, that England had no longer anything to fear from that quarter. They had known that even before the Cleves marriage treaty had been signed. Why then had it been signed? The only answer was Cromwell—it was his doing from first to last, no one else's. Already the need for the Cleves alliance had passed (Norfolk was of the opinion it had never existed) and was proving nothing but a blunder and an embarrassment.

And what about the King and his marriage, saddled to a wife he could not love, with whom he had known the first time he had slept with her he could not have a child? A sad day for England that their sovereign could never have any more children because his minister Cromwell was plotting to bring in Luther's heresies. His Highness himself had not only said how detestable and abominable they were but had written a book against them.

Cromwell, so arrogant in council, so ambitious of others'

blood. Only yesterday he had threatened Norfolk and the Bishops of Winchester, Durham and Bath and Wells, all because he knew they, like their king, hated the new teaching. Norfolk was stout to defend the old faith now their king, whose learning knew no end, had been wise enough to make the Pope the Bishop of Rome. Cromwell and Cranmer would have the whole country Lutheran if they could.

But Norfolk had not only the well-worn string of Cromwell to harp upon. His *bonne bouche,* the feather in his cap, the trick up his sleeve, was his pretty little niece with her red hair, hazel eyes and uptilted nose.

Marillac kept his sovereign posted stage by stage about the English King's affection for another lady, reported to be a great beauty. The Queen was sent to Richmond, and the King promised to follow in two days, but the caustic Marillac predicted his steps would take him in the Lambeth direction instead. They were saying at court that Queen Anne had gone to Richmond of her own accord to remove herself from the plague. Marillac did not believe a word of that tale. If there had been any suspicion of plague in London, the King would have been the first to flee: everyone knew it was the one thing of which he was timid. It was even said that the marriage between him and the young lady of extraordinary beauty had already taken place and was being kept secret. Marillac could not tell how far that report was true.

A deputation instead of her husband waited upon the Queen some three weeks after her arrival at Richmond. Now, Anne knew it was openly said in European courts Henry's first wife had been poisoned; she knew he had beheaded his second and that his third had received an early grave. Before the commissioners could tell her a word of their mission, she, believing they had come to carry her to the Tower, fell to the floor in a dead faint. Her relief was unspeakable when, soothed and com-

210

forted, she was brought round to hear the King's most tender conscience was troubling him again. He did not believe he and she were married. There was that pre-contract of marriage with the Duke of Lorraine that had been made for her when both were minors—the King and his advisers, spiritual and temporal, did not consider it had ever been legally terminated. It was his Majesty's gracious intention to adopt her as a sister; all she would require to do to win that outstanding privilege was to resign the title of Queen. The King would see she would have precedence over every lady at court except his daughters—and of course his future consort. A handsome pension was to be hers, with manors and estates. These were forfeited by Cromwell, now in the Tower on the charge of treason, arrested by Norfolk in the name of the King. And freedom to live abroad or in England, exactly as she chose, although of course if she chose abroad she could neither take her handsome pension nor estates. As for her marriage with the King, it had already been annulled. The nation had to be considered: it had a great interest in their king's having more issue, and the King had never given inward consent to his marriage with her grace, or completed it.

Anne of Cleves had not one objection to raise. She signed the necessary deeds and documents with alacrity and returned Henry's wedding ring in the most affable fashion possible. Never since her arrival in England six months ago had she been happier, holding her own little court. This was her honeymoon without the drawback of a husband swelling visibly with portent and disfavour. Every day she put on a rich new dress of extraordinary fashion from her trousseau.

She took everything in good part, which Marillac said was marvellous prudent of her although some considered it stupidity. Even her recent husband's new bride—she greeted her with acclaim, so glad was she to see another by his side. And when Henry visited her, their meeting was amiable enough to encourage him to stay to sup, when they were merry together as they had never been as husband and wife.

The wedding of the King of England to Katherine Howard took place seven months after his marriage to Anne of Cleves, on the day Cromwell was executed. It was an unproclaimed affair: she was introduced as his wife when she took her seat at chapel beside him. That Sunday she was prayed for in churches throughout the realm as Queen of England.

Never, reported the French ambassador, had he seen the King in such good spirits or in so good a humour. The effect of marriage to his young bride was instantaneous, and love acted on him like elixir. All the buoyancy and vigour of youth returned to him, sending the blood singing in his veins. He was up in the morning at five and hunting until ten, declaring how much better he felt in the country than London. He could not keep his hands from fondling and caressing her, his pretty little nosegay of a bride. Never, he declared, had he been so happily wedded. He chose the rose as her symbol, and called her his rose without a thorn.

CHAPTER SEVENTEEN

BACKSTAIRS SCANDAL

"And, oft before tempestuous winds arise,
 The teeming stars fall headlong from the skies,
 And shooting through the darkness gild the night,
 With sweeping glories, and long trains of light."

THEY came out of the past like beetles from under a stone,
sensitive to change of light; and she was the light. She
heard from the ready writer even before the Anne of
Cleves marriage was annulled, loading her with all the
good wishes of the sender and asking her, once she was
in the Queen's place, to find room for her, "the nearer
I were to you the gladder I would be of it," a letter which
ended that she knew the recipient would not forget her
secretary.

Katherine made her one of her bedchamber women,
and also took into service Katherine Tylney, her cousin,
who had slept with her in the Lambeth dormitory and
shared in the midnight feasts, and Margaret Morton,
another former room-mate. Her one-time music-master,
Manox, is said to have been appointed a royal musician,
and there is no doubt that she employed Dereham as her

usher and secretary for a short time, an act of such folly that it must have been exacted from her to buy his silence.

Dereham had returned to England before her name had been linked with the King's. A young couple were considered married in the eyes of God and the law without engagement or religious ceremony, if they agreed to it between themselves and agreement was accompanied by carnal knowledge. Dereham therefore considered himself and Katherine Howard man and wife, and sought her out to tax her with the court gossip that Thomas Culpeper was to be her husband. Katherine's reply was that he must not trouble her about that "for you know I will not have you". Dereham was not the type to take such a disclaimer lying down, but when the King fell in love with her he did not press his prior claim, although he confided to a friend that if the King were dead he would step into his shoes. As for Thomas Culpeper, he lost no time consoling himself elsewhere and Katherine saw him ingloriously worsted at the jousting celebration to mark her wedding.

The besotted King lavished gifts, jewels, furs and an elaborate household upon his young bride. Never had Katherine dreamed when she yearned for rich stuffs that there were such fabrics in the world and that she should ever be clothed in them. Greedy as a child for the pleasures and sensations of the moment, she was as emotionally unreliable as a demi-mondaine. With all the petting from her royal lover, she grew plump and merry, wearing her clothes, fashioned like a Frenchwoman's, tight about the bodice to reveal her new curves. Marillac voted her face very delightful, and said the King was so enamoured of her he was at a loss to demonstrate his affection. Her motto was "No other than his".

Henry was forty-nine when he took his fifth wife, a panorama of a man, the landscape of his face unfurrowed,

214

the bluff of his brow unlined, the promontory of his nose only beginning to coarsen. And for these idyllic months of early marriage he was able to hold his winter at bay. This was his Indian summer. Something of the old agility returned to that gargantuan frame. In Katherine he recovered his lost youth, when he and life and the world had been at high noontide, and she who brought him this miracle was like a goddess.

He took her to Windsor, dispensing as much as possible with the pomp and restriction of court life while he enjoyed her tirelessness for the round of feasting and dancing, her bubbling naïve pleasure finding herself in his arms, her full red lips to kiss. They made a little progress together, through country towns and landscape yellowing with autumn. The report that a certain Windsor priest, with members of his community, had spoken disrespectfully of the Queen's grace cast no shadow, for the King knew there was no substance behind it. The man was told to confine himself to his own diocese and to be more temperate in the use of his tongue in the future.

Christmas was spent at Hampton Court without the presence of any members of his council to disturb with business a festival elate with present happiness and past childhood memories. Amongst the gifts he bestowed on his bride were a diamond and ruby brooch edged with pearls and a muffler of black velvet furred with sables and gemmed with rubies and hundreds of pearls. Rubies were fitting to give one whose price was far above them, and whose husband praised her. He went up to London to see to business in the New Year but returned in three days after he had transacted it.

It was during Lent that the first ruffle appeared on the placid waters of the eight-month marriage. The King had an attack of fever which left him irascible and melancholy. The ulcer on his leg flared again, distorting his face with

215

pain, and when he could manage to walk he had to hobble miserably on a stick.

Physical disability cracked the delusion that he could put the clock back. His Golden Age had not returned. News of a small rising in the north raised his choler and deepened his depression although this time it was abortive, stamped out almost before it had begun. He said he had an evil people to rule. The very youth of his inconsequential wife irked him, and for over a week he refused to see her. Instead of a royal bridegroom, Katherine came face to face with a frightening, obese, quarrelsome man, sagging into gloom or shouting with rage.

She beguiled the tedium of these days while the King lay sick amusing herself with Thomas Culpeper who, as gentleman of the privy chamber, was about the court. When she gave him a velvet cap garnished with a jewelled brooch, she told him to put it under his cloak that nobody would see it. And she wrote him the only letter of hers in existence, a love letter: she was not literate like Katherine of Aragon or Anne Boleyn, but wrote and expressed herself like a child.

As soon as Henry could resume his normal activities he did, flouting his doctors. The belief that Katherine was with child cheered him and he determined, if it proved true, to have her crowned at Whitsuntide. Unfortunately it was a false surmise, so his little Queen forfeited her coronation for the present. But the rising in the north had reminded him of his promise five years ago during the Pilgrimage of Grace negotiations that he would make a progress to that unvisited quarter of his realm.

Arrangements were at once put in hand, for the planning and provisioning of such an undertaking was prodigious. This was to be no ordinary progress: Henry was not only going to show himself to his seditious subjects as their king but what manner of king he was. His whole court ac-

216

companied him, and it took two hundred tents to house them alone, also nearly all his council. The barbaric north was to be dazzled by the choicest royal tapestries, the finest plate and the King's richest wardrobe, and impressed by the size of the army marching alongside. The enormous cavalcade included five thousand horses to carry men and supplies. Eighty archers with drawn bows preceded them when they entered a city.

It was a life that suited Henry, constant movement to absorb his tremendous energies, the strong northern air, the stimulus of new scenes and sights. This was his realm although he had never set foot on it before, these forests of oak, wastes of scrub, brushwood and thickets, moorland and mossland where grey sheep cropped, their tangled wool parted by the wind; each town fringed with fields and run-rigs of land wrested from the wilderness surrounding it. Standing on its rocky height, his keep or castle awaited him, their grey walls tough to withstand the assault and battering-ram of storm and man.

And these were his subjects. His keen huntsman's eye glinted over them whose fathers and fathers' fathers had fought for the white rose of York against the red. They were bigger than the men in the south, their features craggy and projecting from their faces, which made them look like the corbel heads in his father's chapel. Yes, these were his subjects, whether he or they liked it or not.

He sent proclamation before him that if any found themselves grieved for lack of justice, they were to have full access to declare their complaints to him, that they could have right dealt them at the hand of his Majesty. Hard on the proclamation followed his Majesty in person, formidable with bulk, not like a man as they were men, but powerful as the State, iron-bound as the Law, sacrosanct as the Church, their anointed king.

It was triumph all the way for Henry, extending his

royal pardon, accepting humble submission from kneeling civic authorities, receiving expiatory gifts and propitiating bags of gold at every halt.

He reached the walled city of York in the middle of September, his health recovered, jocund and active, supervising the construction of a vast lodging outside the city. At first it was thought he intended to have his Queen crowned in York Minster, whose pale stone glowed with the gold of past summers. But soon it was discovered this was to be the scene of another Field of Cloth of Gold, not so spectacular of course, although Henry marshalled all the resources at hand to make a fine display, but a rendezvous that would, he felt, bear more lasting fruit.

Instead of Francis I of France, his counterpart this time was to be James V of Scotland, who had promised to ride across the border and hold tryst with his uncle and neighbour King. Their meeting would be a worthy climax to a progress that had been a paean of satisfaction. Henry had no doubts that he had but to meet his nephew to prove to him that his uncle's friendship was more valuable than the French King's.

Greenwich, Hatfield, Lincoln, Pontefract, York—the summer months swung by for Katherine, dressing herself in different dresses of crimson velvet except when she entered a city, when her gowns were of silver. She was Queen of the England she was passing through, second to none but her lord and sovereign, receiving homage, adulation and honour every mile of the way, and it was not enough. Satiated with plenty, she hungered for forbidden fruit.

Her principal lady-in-waiting was Lady Rochford, who had kept her position at court throughout the reigns of Anne Boleyn, Jane Seymour and Anne of Cleves. She had been the wife of George Boleyn, against whom she had borne witness, a woman with an obsession for playing with fire and edge tools. She now acted as intermediary between the young Queen and presentable young Thomas Culpeper, carrying messages, arranging assignations late at night, the only one to be present with the Queen when he came lurking up the backstairs.

"Jesus! is not the Queen abed yet?" Katherine Tylney asked Margaret Morton one hot night at Lincoln when their mistress was still in Lady Rochford's room at two o'clock. The doors were barred from the inside at Pontefract once the King came to spend the night with his wife, and there was some delay before he was admitted. None of the Queen's attendants ever saw or heard who was supposed to be closeted with her and Lady Rochford, but she betrayed her infatuation for Culpeper to her servants simply by the way she looked and spoke to him in daily intercourse.

His royal uncle waited twelve days at York for James who did not come; the French party were in ascendancy in Scotland and his nephew begged to be excused. Henry was very angry indeed. Instead of blandishing the Tudor charm, he had to prepare for his return journey. The great pavilion was taken down which was to have staged history in the making, the tapestries rolled up, the plate carried away whose richness was guaranteed to make any Scot blink. Throughout the journey back Henry was vocal on the subject of his nephew, rumbling with threats of vengeance.

But this disappointment was the one discordant note in the whole progress. When he arrived home at Hampton Court towards the end of October he, touched and gratified by the humility and devotion of his northern subjects, was at peace with himself and all the world. Those members of his council, including Cranmer, who had been in charge of the government in his absence, were there to welcome him.

On All Hallows Day a mass of thanksgiving took place for the safe return of the King's Grace. He expressed his gratitude to his Maker for the good life he was leading and trusted to lead with his present Queen after the troubles he had suffered through his earlier marriages. He was a ship that across tempestuous seas at last reaches haven, and he instructed his confessor to make like prayer publicly and give like thanks with him.

Twenty-four hours later as he left his private chapel, Cranmer handed him a letter, thrusting it at him in his importunity to be rid of it, requesting him in a low voice to read it in private.

The Archbishop told through his pen what he could not say to his King by word of mouth. The Queen upon whom his affection was so marvellously set had lived most corruptly and sensually.

Sometimes an avalanche can be caused by the dislodgement of a pebble. One John Lassels said to his sister Mary, a servant of Duchess Agnes who had shared the dormitory with her granddaughters, why did she not ask for a place in the Queen's household as the others had done? Mary replied she had no wish to enter the Queen's service, but she pitied her. "Why so?" inquired her brother. "Marry!" came the reply, "because she is light both in conditions and living."

John Lassels was a fervid Protestant, and religious zeal would not permit him to sleep on such disclosures. He asked for an interview with the Archbishop of Canterbury, well known for his Protestant leanings. Immediately aware of the weight and importance of what he had heard, Cranmer relayed it at once to his two fellow council members who had not gone, like Norfolk, on the northern progress.

The conclusion arrived at was inevitable: the King must be told. The scandal was not unwelcome for it offered an opportunity of undermining the Howard predominance at court, but no one wanted the painful duty of being the one to tell him. They knew his anger. It could rend and tear apart anyone who dared reveal what the love of his heart and the light of his eye really was. It was Cranmer who undertook to write and deliver the letter. He was probably motivated by his duty to his royal master more than the others, who seized the chance to bring about the downfall of the Duke of Norfolk and the Roman Catholic party.

The King's reaction was totally different from what anyone had expected. He did not tower with rage. He was not disturbed, except that the calumny against Katherine should be investigated and the perpetrators punished. Not a word of it did he believe. He had only to look at his bride of little more than a year with the bloom of youth and the dew of freshness upon her to be assured. He had lived long enough in the world to know all about the malice on idle and lying tongues. Quietly he ordered that no stone should be left unturned to discover the falsity of the rumours, and continued in high spirits for the rest of the week.

On the Sunday morning, 6th November, 1541, Henry attended in person at Hampton Court a full meeting of his council, an unusual proceeding; but the circumstances were unusual and he had to learn the siftings of the scandals against his Queen that appropriate punishments might be dispensed.

Instead he heard proof after proof of her looseness before her marriage. Mary Lassels said Manox, the music-teacher, knew a private mark on Katherine's body. Manox admitted guilty familiarity with her but said Dereham had supplanted him in her affections. Dereham confessed he and Katherine had had intercourse but there was no guilt in it as their precontract made her his wife.

They saw the King age as they looked at him when dis-

221

belief at last gave up the struggle. For a moment he was a giant again, shouting for a sword with which to slay the girl who had betrayed him and swearing that she would never have such delight in her incontinency as she would have torture in her death. As suddenly he collapsed, like a tower whose foundations have shifted, and they turned their faces away not to see their king weeping, a strange sight in one of his courage.

The man who left the council chamber was not the same as the man who had entered it. He was never to be the same again. Time at last made up on him, vanquishing all the magniloquence of youth, and the greyness of age took root. He rode to London that afternoon, taking a few musicians with him and without saying where he was going.

Cranmer, with four members of the council, visited Katherine's apartments and accused her of failing to disclose her immorality before she married the King. Throughout all the lengthy inquisitions and interrogations that were to follow she acted true to her type, extenuations depriving too full confessions of their content, her defence weakened by deception, crawling remorse overridden by the anxiety to remove the blame to her partners. Unable to extricate herself from the ever-developing situation, she unconsciously took refuge in hysteria. That Sunday night it was thought she would lose her reason.

A gallery at Hampton Court is still called the haunted gallery because it is said her ghost frequents it. That Sunday, knowing the King would be at mass in his chapel, she tried to reach him but was caught and forced back to her apartments. Her shrieks tearing up and down the gallery are said to echo there today.

Cranmer was instructed on the Monday to bring home to the Queen how grievously she had offended, to make much of the punishment she deserved, and then to inform her the King was graciously pleased to pardon her and remit these dread punishments. Instead she was to be degraded from the rank of Queen and confined in custody.

Seeing the condition Katherine was in, Cranmer wisely told her about the pardon first, which steadied her to a certain extent. Taken off her guard the day before, she had instinctively denied everything with all the strength she could summon. Now she admitted that she had allowed him, through flattery and fair persuasions on the part of Manox, to take liberties with her, and confessed that Dereham by many persuasions procured her for his vicious purposes. But she would not agree there was anything like a precontract between them, as that would have made it even more heinous for her to have gone through a form of marriage with the King of England when she knew she was already married to Francis Dereham. Also she had for long wanted not to be tied to but finished with him.

Questioned whether she had ever called him husband and he her wife, she had to agree that happened many times. She supposed it was true that at one time he kissed her very often, and that once when some spectators remarked on it, he answered, "Who should hinder me from kissing my own wife?" But she slipped through the questioners' net each time by saying she had not appreciated such behaviour constituted marriage.

When she thought of what she had lost and for what, Katherine could not contain her grief and remorse. Even through her statement of guilt addressed to the King, sufficient in itself to warrant the death penalty, there emerges a picture of the man to whom she is writing as she remembers him, his unfailing goodness, always so gracious and loving a prince to her.

The news that a second niece of his had proved herself an unworthy escort for the King struck the Duke of Norfolk like a thunderbolt. He wrote at once to Henry beseeching him to forgive him the sins of his seditious family and to continue his good and gracious Lord. Katherine's unchastity before her marriage may have been and probably was hidden from her uncle, but to prove his shock and horror he had to draw attention to them. He disowned all his relations sent to the Tower who had known of Katherine's past, uncovered incriminating evidence against his stepmother, Duchess Agnes, who had commended her granddaughter to the King as worthy of the honour to be his wife; accompanied Cranmer on several occasions to interrogate the degraded Queen; and as he sat with the rest of the council at the male prisoners' trial, laughed loudly when the prosecution scored a point. He was all for having his "ungrateful niece" burned alive for her sins.

It was the King who showed patience and some compassion. Katherine Howard's treatment was gentle compared to that meted out to Anne Boleyn. It was carefully stipulated that her keys were not to be taken from her, which meant that she could move about her rooms with some freedom, and she was to choose four gentlewomen and two chamberers as her attendants. But her jewels were taken from her, all cloth of state removed and her most sumptuous dresses.

Cranmer broke up the Queen's household at Hampton Court, and she was sent under guard to the suppressed monastery of Syon. Believing the worst was over, the enormity of her faults and sins diminished to more conventional size, and she became cheerful again. She dressed herself from her restricted wardrobe as carefully as she had done when she was Queen and was said to be plump and pretty as ever. But it was noticed she was more imperious and difficult to please than she had been when she was the King's wife.

The Council determined to suppress, quite illegally, the precontract evidence because it would assist the defence. Their difficulty was Dereham could not be found guilty of having lain with his wife either before or after her marriage to the King, and Dereham must be inculpated. Accused of having renewed their former intercourse during the short space he was the Queen's secretary, he, to prove himself innocent, protested that Culpeper had succeeded him in the Queen's affections.

Thomas Culpeper, gentleman-in-waiting, favourite at court! They were after the new scent in full cry. The unsuspecting gallant was apprehended while he was hawking, and Katherine was questioned about her relationship with him.

She admitted the backstairs assignations as did Culpeper, who added the detail that the Queen, not unnaturally, was in great fear lest somebody should come in. Katherine even confessed to calling him her little sweet fool and giving him a cap and a ring, but both he and she denied adultery. Her explanation of the midnight meetings was Culpeper wanted them and they had been engineered by Lady Rochford for some dark reasons of her own.

Lady Rochford's evidence was verbose but contradictory. She had never wanted to act as go-between, but the Queen and Culpeper forced her to it. She had never heard what the Queen and Culpeper said to each other, but thought Culpeper must have known the Queen carnally, considering all the things she had heard and seen between them.

Both Culpeper and Dereham were tortured although torture was illegal in England. There was no one to question the persecution (Katherine had no trial); if so, their answer would have been that in a case that involved the royal person of the King all means were lawful. Both men refused to confess, even on the rack, they had committed misconduct with the Queen after her marriage. But Katherine's doom was sealed as well as his own when Culpeper admitted he intended and meant to do ill with her and that in like wise she so minded to do with him.

This woman had been Queen of England, this woman might, but for the grace of God, have borne a son during the short time she shared the King's bed. She and her lovers had committed the worst crime that could be committed; they had confounded the succession.

Not bigamy but adultery! His young wife had made a cuckold of him. He might be King of England but to her he was an old man. He who had believed Henry Tudor was not like the common run, that his place could never be filled as long as he drew breath, saw himself displanted by nincompoops who could only boast their youth.

Both Culpeper and Dereham asked to be beheaded instead of the traitor's death of hanged, drawn and quartered. The King granted the boon to Culpeper but not to Dereham.

Lady Rochford was executed on the same day as her young mistress. Her mind gave under the ceaseless questioning; she had probably been streaked with insanity all along, and a bill was brought in that the State could proceed against those who had lost their reason. However, she made the conventional "good death" of exhortation, edification and repentance, although one observer did feel she took too long cataloguing her offences. One of these was that she had brought this shameful death upon herself because of having contributed to her husband's fate by her false accusation of Queen Anne Boleyn.

Parliament saved the King the pain of signing the Queen's death warrant. It also brought in an Act which declared it treason for any woman to marry the King if her previous life had been unchaste. "Few, if any, ladies now at court would henceforth aspire to that honour," was Chapuys's comment to that.

Katherine was taken from Syon to the Tower. She knew what lay before her, but as she was being escorted to the barge and saw the galleys that were to escort it, she would have turned. Struggling, she was put on board.

The night before she was to die she asked that the block be brought into her cell so that she might learn how to place her head on it. On the day of her execution her brother and cousin paraded themselves, making merry and ostentatiously dressed in festival finery, in the streets of London. "It is the custom," the laconic Marillac noted, "and must be done to show they did not share the crimes of their relatives."

No man chose death rather than say Katherine Howard was not guilty as four did for the sake of Anne Boleyn. No stories reach us of the love her ladies-in-waiting bore her as they bore her elder cousin. No token of hers was handed down from generation to generation like the one Anne Boleyn gave on her execution morning to the officer on guard because of his unfailing respectful conduct towards her. Katherine Howard stands almost alone in that she has no mourners, unless she was remembered in the heart of an ageing king.

Henry had to carry the knowledge that what was said against Anne Boleyn, except the incest, was true of Katherine Howard. What he would have given to have heard a Dereham or a Culpeper proclaim he would rather die a thousand deaths than accuse the Queen of what he knew her to be innocent. Instead, to save themselves, they had placed the blame at her door as she had at theirs.

The King seemed very old and grey to Marillac when he next saw him; he reported he took such grief that of late it was thought he had gone mad, and Chapuys wrote that he had been low-spirited ever since he heard of the late Queen's misconduct.

CHAPTER EIGHTEEN

THE LAST BARGAIN

"This ae nighte, this ae nighte,
  Everie nighte and alle,
Fire and sleet and candle-light,
  And Christe receive thy saule."

WHILE Henry was on his northern progress, his son Edward fell ill with a quartan fever. He was four years old and his portraits confirm the reports that he was a handsome boy, blond and broad-browed like his father. There is a cameo which represents them both; Henry's arm is round his shoulder, clamping him to him like a lion its cub. But although the boy recovered from the ague, it left him delicate, and his doctors realized that after all he had not inherited his parent's constitution, while his pictures began to portray him still good-looking but fragile and thin. Highly intelligent, like all Henry's children, from the beginning he took the liveliest interest in all that was going on around him. He was a scholarly boy who played the lute, was thrilled by the stars, and learnt Latin, Greek, French and Italian. Beloved by his father's people, they called him England's Treasure.

News that his sister Margaret had died in Scotland reached Henry when he was restlessly moving from place to place as his councillors inquired into the abominable demeanour of his Queen. Margaret, older than he, had never meant to him what his younger sister Mary had, but her death coming at such a time depressed him. Now he alone was left. He sent to learn whether his sister was really dead and if she had left a will.

The clouds that had threatened so long at last broke into open warfare between England and Scotland. The northern country was an irritant to Henry who became more and more impatient as he grew older. He could not induce James to break with Rome (his uncle's suggestion that he should imburse himself by despoiling the monasteries struck the Scots King as blasphemous, although like most men, and all kings, he liked well to be rich), and Scotland's ancient alliance with France made her a source of potential danger to her English neighbour.

The first round went to James, whose success over his uncle greatly elated him. Henry ordered Norfolk to avenge the defeat, issued a plausible manifesto regretting he was compelled to use arms against his nephew, and sent a warning to James that he still had the same rod in his keeping which had chastised his father.

Norfolk entered Scotland on his punitive expedition with twenty thousand men. The Scots side of the border was a much richer country than the English side, which meant the English could wreak immeasurably more harm quicker when they crossed into Scotland than the Scots could when they crossed into the barren bog and harsh moorland that edged England. Another Scottish disadvantage was their capital of Edinburgh was within easy striking distance of the border, whereas London was buried deep in England.

It was October and the harvest garnered in what was the granary of Scotland. Norfolk reduced it to ashes, and sacked and fired farms, villages, towns and abbeys along the Tweed. He had no intention of making organized war; it was far too late in the year for that, and after inflicting as much damage as he could, as a lesson to the Scots for not complying with his master, he wheeled his army and made to fall back on his home country.

The cry from the borders reached the Scots King who, hot to invade England, pursued the enemy with thirty thousand men; but when the tide of battle could have turned in his favour, his nobles, whose disaffection was chronic, withdrew their support. They allowed the English to cross safely over the Tweed, and dispersed to their homes.

James had been King of Scotland for the twenty-nine of his thirty years, having inherited the crown when his father was killed at Flodden. He had the Stewart red hair, oval face, heavy lids, and above all the Stewart blood, with its mixture of charm and passion, its wayward weakness allied to great nobility, and its undiluted personal courage. He made a good ruler to his people, but his nobles were too strong, too lawless, too factious, to be subdued: the only counter he had to keep them in check was the Church. For four years he had been married to French Marie of Guise, whom his uncle had wanted and whom he had won, and she had borne him two sons, both of whom had died within a few days of each other. James began to show signs of his grandfather's melancholy and could not sleep. Now his Queen wife was in Linlithgow Palace for her third lying-in.

It was the Church which provided him with another army after his nobles' defection, and the King marched west with it where he fell ill. It was now November, too late for warfare, but James may well have reasoned that it was better to use an army when he had one to use. Too sick to lead the men himself, he made the disastrous decision of sending them forward into enemy country.

The Scottish force crossed the Esk during the night. The men believed the King was with them and only discovered he was not when dawn broke over the flats of the treacherous Solway Moss. Dissension broke out as to who was to lead and into the confusion rode an English force a quarter their number.

This had none of the heart-breaking heroism of Flodden. This was panic, rout, abject defeat. Hundreds of high-ranking prisoners were taken by the English. News of the disaster was carried to the sick Scots King. He had one more blow to sustain before he succumbed, when he heard on his death-bed before the end of the year that his queen was safely delivered—of a daughter. Crying out, "The deil take it! The deil take it!" he turned his face to the wall. The child he never saw was Mary, Queen of Scots before she was a week old.

Henry saw in the birth of his great-niece at her father's death providence working for him, and he seized the opportunity in his strenuous hands. There was another process now than costly warfare by which the Scots crown could be seized—marriage. It had been tried before; each king, except his father, who had sat on the English throne had attempted to subject Scotland through either conquest or marriage, but never had such an opportunity as this presented itself, with so many influential prisoners to play their part in Henry's game. And throughout this game played without rules, he never lost sight of the ball, the small Scots Queen.

Union of marriage must be effected between the newborn Queen and Prince Edward—on Henry's terms. He sold their freedom to the Solway prisoners on condition they agreed, on their return, to have the child straightway delivered to his guardianship. But it was one thing to promise the King of England everything he demanded on English soil, another to fulfil their promises on their return when the mother of the proposed bride was a

Frenchwoman and their fellow Scots had no intention of selling either their country or their Queen to their hereditary enemies.

The best the Solway lords could achieve for the English monarch was that Mary should be espoused to Edward and sent to England in her tenth year. Henry had to modify his terms which he did with a poor grace, for the Scots saw to it that the marriage treaty left no loophole for annexation. One Scots nobleman voiced what all his countrymen were thinking when he said, "I dislike not so much the marriage as the manner of the wooing."

If Henry had been content, as he would have been content earlier, with the marriage of the Scots Queen to his son, all the patient and skilled negotiations of his former years might well have borne fruit. His deteriorating health contributed something to his diminishing statesmanship where Scotland was concerned, but he had grown into a despot and despotism and conciliation do not go hand in hand. He had completed the union of Wales with England and was now King of Ireland. Scotland alone prevented his title to Emperor of Great Britain, and the possibility of a British Empire was ruled out so long as his weaker but stubborn neighbour had the aid of rich and powerful France.

Francis at present had his hands full as he had declared war on Charles when their ten-year-old friendship had still six years to run. When it suited Henry he concluded an alliance with Charles and declared war on Francis, ostensibly to recover his ancient rights in France and because Francis had committed the unpardonable sin against Christendom by giving entry into Europe to the hordes of infidel Turk, but in reality to destroy the support which enabled Scotland to resist union with England.

The wheel had turned full circle, the three powers were back where they had been at the start of their reigns: Spain and England versus France.

Francis could not believe it. When Henry's ambassador presented him with his letters of recall, the French King spoke of the English sovereign as his good brother, his best brother, his best beloved brother who assuredly could not be his enemy. He offered liberal terms if Henry would make a separate peace with him, but Henry kept his pledge to Charles. Francis, who was gaining ally after ally with every victory against the morose Emperor, was his rival as Charles would never be.

Seventeen months after the execution of his fifth wife, Henry married his sixth, Katherine Parr. She was aged thirty-one and had been twice widowed. Their wedding was no hole-and-corner affair like those of the Howard cousins but took place at Hampton Court with all due observances, in the presence of his two daughters, although without the pageantry that marked that to Anne of Cleves. But this was no political union to impress the world; it was the marriage of a sick king in need of a helpmeet.

On the 12th July, 1543, in the Queen's closet, the bride, in love with another man who was to be her fourth husband, promised, "I Katherine, take thee, Henry, to my wedded husband, to have and to hold from this day forward, for better for worse, for richer for poorer, in sickness and in health, to be bonair and buxom in bed and at board, till death us do part."

The woman who stood beside her sovereign and husband that day was small in stature, with a serene brow and hazel eyes, her features delicately clear cut as those on a miniature. A contemporary Spanish chronicler tells us she was quieter than any of the young wives the King had had, and as she knew more of the world got on well with him, and had no caprices. But, he adds, she kept her ladies very strictly, perhaps no bad thing when the histories of recent ladies-in-waiting are considered.

The man who stood beside her was fifty-two years old,

unwieldy with corpulence, his small eyes needling in his stoutening face. His sands of time were running out; he had not four years to live, but magnificence still clung to him: it was his person—not the monstrous body one saw on his wedding-day—amiable and benign on so pleasant an occasion.

The only tart comment on the marriage came from Henry's fourth wife in her contented if retired little court. Anne of Cleves was a prudent housewife, generous to her servants, who remained throughout on affectionate terms with Mary and Elizabeth, Henry's daughters. When she heard of her former husband's sixth essay at wedlock she remarked, "A fine burthen Madam Katherine has taken on herself."

The fine burden never shut the door against Katherine Parr as he had against some of his former wives. Her soothing presence was always welcome to him. She was not afraid of him when, goaded with pain, he raged and blamed. Something of the tenor of life with Katherine of Aragon returned with Katherine Parr, although circumstances were as different as age from youth, but both women were tender, tactful, humane, and in their devotion put him first not so much because he was their sovereign but because he was their husband.

Another characteristic his new English wife shared with her Spanish counterpart was both were learned. His marriage to Katherine Howard had swung the religious balance towards the Catholic side, his last marriage swayed it towards the Reformers. Katherine Parr liked to discuss theological subjects, and was earnest for reform. Once her tongue ran away with her to such an extent that Henry considered she was poaching on his preserves. He was heard to mutter what were things coming to when women turned priests and he in his old days was taught by his wife. It never happened again. At once Katherine said it would be unbecoming in her to assert opinions contrary to those of her lord; her remarks were only intended to minister talk. "Is it so, Sweetheart?" he replied, "then we are perfect friends."

At first Henry directed the course of hostilities with France from his court. He dispatched a general with the resounding name of Wallop at the head of six thousand troops to reinforce Charles's army in the Netherlands, while he tried to raise money to pay for a war that had scarcely begun and whose cost was already reaching astronomical sums. As his father's fortune had long ago disappeared, so had the one accumulated for him by Cromwell. A hard-pressed King levied forced loans, debased the coinage, sold crown lands and raised loans in the Netherlands at ruinous rates of interest, while his people asked in their grumbling way what were they gaining fighting France except exposure to war on two fronts.

The ink was hardly dry on the marriage and peace treaties with Scotland than the bridegroom's father seized Scots merchant ships in his high-handed way. Edinburgh rose. The Enlgish envoy escaped only in the nick of time when the house where he lodged was burnt down by the populace. He wrote to Henry complaining of the beastly liberties the Scots enjoyed, concluding with the remark that he would rather be among Turks. Hastily the Scots arranged the coronation of their Queen. The ceremony, performed with crown, sceptre, sword and baby, exacerbated Henry. The Scots declared the English treaties null and void, and renewed their alliance with France.

It was more than Henry would tolerate. Determined to be Mary's father-in-law, he sent an army into Scotland to take her by force. His instructions, which were carried out to the letter, were to inflict all the misery it could, lay waste to the country, and put to fire and sword man, woman and child. The royal child was hurried from one stronghold to another before the destructive arm of the

236

English King, who with every blow strengthened the French party in Scotland. The army returned to England, leaving desolation in its wake, but without the bride or beating Scotland to its knees.

Henry was very ill that year, suffering severe pain and fever caused by his sore leg. The ulceration was not syphillitic in origin but varicose, the veins on his leg becoming plugged or thrombosed. He would sit with it on his wife's lap, or lie in bed disputing with his doctors.

Nothing would stop him crossing the Channel to lead his army in person against the French King. His physicians said it was madness, his Council was horrified and even Charles sent a special envoy to dissuade him. The envoy arrived and was given audience by the King, whom he found so determined upon the voyage he did not dare attempt to dissuade him. Henry boasted his strong and robust constitution enabled him to stand illness, but the ambassador noted his face clearly showed he was much worse than he was making out.

Henry arranged with Charles, who was to invade France from the north-west, to effect a junction with their armies and together march on Paris. In July he sailed from Dover to Calais in a ship with sails of cloth of gold. With him went his new armour, as he had outgrown his old, and a heavy charger specially selected and trained to carry his increased bulk.

Sometimes he had to be borne on a litter and to leave his troops to Suffolk, old now but his ablest general, and Norfolk, older still and not so successful on foreign soil as he was on home ground. But Henry was an old campaigner, and amongst men, horses and arms he felt strong and more than able for the stir, clatter and challenge of battle. He camped in torrents of rain and thunder and spent all day in the fields.

The English sat down to besiege Boulogne, which upset Charles, who wanted them to meet him as soon as possible striking west. But Boulogne was a prize Henry had been done out of twenty-one years ago, when Wolsey and his imperial allies had prevailed on him to forego it, and twenty-one years was a long time to wait for Henry to get something on which he had set his heart.

He and Charles might be on enemy soil as allies but neither was in the least interested in the other's objects for going to war, only in his own. While Henry besieged Boulogne and Charles St. Dizier, Francis's envoys were working overtime trying to drive a wedge between them by plying each with separate olive branches and tempting concessions. Henry informed Charles most sedulously of all French peace-feelers, which he loftily spurned, but the reticent Charles was not so forthcoming.

In the agreeable letters Henry wrote home we catch echoes of those he wrote thirty-one years ago to Katherine of Aragon in the same circumstances. He told his wife how busy he had been, seeing and caring for everything. In September he broke the good news that the outworks of the castle had been taken under his command, and the French were unlikely to recover them again (after this sentiment he appended "so we trust" in brackets). Progress was delayed because provision of powder had not come out of Flanders as expected, but he had no doubt that, with God's grace, castle and town would follow the same trade. "No more to you at this time, Sweetheart, but for lack of time and great occupation of business, saving, we pray you, to give in our name our hearty blessings to all our children. . . . Written with the hand of your loving husband, Henry R."

It might have been Katherine of Aragon holding the pen when Katherine Parr wrote of the capture of a Scots ship at Rye, with many Frenchmen as well as Scots on board, bearing letters to the French King which she had examined and was sending the most important to him; also any further information which could be extracted from the prisoners. Although it was not many days since he departed, yet already it seemed a long time to her who felt the want of his presence. She told him my lord Prince and the rest of his children were all, thanks to God, in very good health, concluding "Your Grace's most humble loving wife and servant".

Katherine was a tender stepmother to the three children and while Henry was abroad the family lived together, for the most part at Hampton Court. All three loved, looked up to and patterned themselves on their gifted stepmother. Edward copied her beautiful handwriting, and the way she expressed herself made him think how poor were his own compositions. She encouraged Mary and Elizabeth to translate passages from the Scriptures, and each compiled a little manual of devotions in Latin, French and English and dedicated it to her.

There were only a few years between Mary, aged twenty-eight, and Katherine Parr. Not even their different religious emphasis separated them; indeed at her stepmother's instigation Mary undertook the translation of a Reformer's Latin paraphrase of St. John.

The last few years of Henry's life, while he was married to his sixth wife, mark a pleasant interlude on Mary's calendar. Her father, even had he so desired, could not will away the crown from his legitimate son, but he could pronounce who was to inherit it in the event of Edward's death. Failing Edward, it was to fall to Mary; failing Mary and her heirs, to Elizabeth. Neither sister wished their adored little brother to die, but the fact that they were accepted in the direct line of succession made a difference to their prestige and circumstances.

Mary's love of flowers did not begin and end there. She made a study of them, and delighted in rare seeds and roots brought from abroad—to watch a Spanish plant establish itself in English soil. It was Spain, her mother's country, that she loved. She had her collection of clocks and dogs (Italian greyhounds were her favourites), and a pet white lark.

At twenty-eight she was still unmarried. Two years ago, when relations between Francis and Henry were more cordial, there was talk and even negotiations about marrying her to the Duke of Orleans, Francis's second son, but the fathers could not agree on the dowry. Francis demanded a million crowns, Henry coolly offered 200,000, saying that was fair enough because the Duke was but a second son. The French ambassador heaved twenty sighs, cast his eyes up to heaven as many times and crossed himself. Henry was told the French would rather take the lady Mary in her kirtle than a mean 200,000 crowns, and the alliance fell through like all the others. Mary was like one of her own seeds kept too long which never flourished as it should.

Her half-sister Elizabeth was eleven. She had not the fair skin of Henry's other children but was sallow like her mother, and her eyes had some of Anne Boleyn's beauty. Already she knew she had pretty hands and took care that others noticed them. She was going to be tall, and whereas Mary was always ailing she was spirited and strong. She was as well educated as her elder sister, without the same need for application and study, so that later she was to carry her learning with panache. In temperament she was far more like her father than was Mary; so like, indeed, that sometimes their contact had the action of metal against metal. He had been so angry with Elizabeth shortly after his last marriage that he had refused to see her or permit her to write to him for a whole year, and had passed over to France without a sign that he knew of her existence. But Katherine was waging her pen adroitly on her young stepdaughter's behalf, and her father's message to *all* his children showed Elizabeth she was forgiven. She was eloquent with gratitude to her stepmother for having brought about the reconciliation.

Boulogne surrendered in September, and Henry had the glory of entering the city at the head of his troops. Now he was ready to join up with Charles for their march on Paris. But Charles, in a tight corner with his army endangered, was convinced Boulogne was all that Henry wanted and that the English would never advance to support him. So, five days after it fell, he made a separate peace with Francis.

It had happened all over again, what had happened more than once in the past. England's Spanish ally had left her in the lurch. As the campaigning season was now far advanced and sickness had broken out among his troops, there was nothing for Henry to do but return home, leaving his prize of Boulogne strongly fortified.

The winter passed uneasy with portent. Henry told Chapuys he was ten times better at Boulogne than he had been since, and the ambassador described him as much broken since his return. Even Henry could not get away with the enormous demands he made on his physical strength. In February the Scots with a small force defeated an English army, and Francis, liberated from war with Charles, prepared to launch an armada on England.

The hour his enemies had promised themselves had at last struck for Henry VIII. He stood alone, without an ally in the world, the Scots victorious in the north, the French about to descend on him from the south. Now his people would rise up against their excommunicate King who had brought them to this pass, their prosecutor, a blood-thirsty tyrant, the enemy of the Church. Seventy-two thousand persons were said to have been put to death during his reign; if that were so it was nearly two and a half per cent of the total population of England. Their blood cried out for vengeance on their slayer.

But his people did not rise against him. Their King was coining his plate and mortgaging his estates for their defence; surely they could pay loans, subsidies and benevolences to help him. He had always seen to the defences of the country from the beginning, inspecting them himself to see they were kept in repair. They must say that for him. He had built castles of granite on the coast especially to accommodate artillery. There was really no one like him, their King. Look at the fleet he had built; as long as any of them could remember he had been adding ships to it. No, there wasn't a king in the whole world equal to him. Only he could go over to France and take a city like Boulogne from under the Frenchies' noses. They say his Council wanted him to strike a bargain with the French King, sell Boulogne back to him for a fortune, and save us trying to victual and garrison it on enemy soil. But he wouldn't hear of that, not their good King Hal. He wouldn't let a prize like that out of his hands. Neither would we. After all, we've the ships to provision it, haven't we? We're like our King, we'd rather spend all we had and risk everything to keep a trophy like Boulogne.

Spring brought the invading ships from France, two hundred of them. Henry's much vaunted fleet of half their number seemed very small in comparison. Some foreign soldiers landed but when the English destroyed a bridge so that they could not cross, they appeared undecided what to do. Enemy ships tried to force their way into Portsmouth harbour but French navigators knew nothing about the swirl of English contending tides or native hidden sandbanks, and the attempt failed. God was most certainly on the side of the English, for a westerly breeze sprang up from nowhere and the French had to drop down before it along the Sussex coast.

Henry's *Mary Rose* sank with all hands on board, but that was the one disaster. English ships followed the French and the two fleets anchored for the night almost within gunshot. There was no engagement the following day for there was no enemy to engage. When the light of dawn pierced the sky, it revealed the horizon swallowing the last French ship as their fleet lurched back to home waters. Disease had broken out on board and taken such toll there was hardly a soldier fit to bear arms. Yes, God was on Henry's side. He always had been and always would to the end of the chapter.

Henry saw Katherine wore as many wonderful jewels as her slight form could carry when plenipotentiaries arrived from France to discuss peace. It was the New Year and the entertainment of the foreign dignitaries made resplendent the grey chill of January. But for all their splendour, there was something of afterglow about the festivities, for they were the last ever to gild Henry's court.

The treaty was favourable to him in every respect. England was to hold Boulogne and district for eight years, when France was to redeem it for two million crowns. France was to resume paying Henry his pension (the clause to have it back-dated was the only one Henry waived), and help him to force the Scots to renew the marriage and peace pacts they had declared null and void.

He, the King of half an island, was recognized as an equal in Europe by Francis and Charles. But the world scene was changing; characters who had dominated the stage for so long had played out their parts. There were others ready to take over their roles waiting in the wings, that limbo draughty with the past, shuffling with the present, empty of the future.

Henry VIII, Francis I and Charles V—Henry had only a year to live, Francis little more. The solitary Charles was not like the two rivals, competing for the centre of the stage, cutting in on the other's lines. He did not wait for his cue from death to force him, still talking, to make his exit, but resigned one crown after another before retiring to a monastery.

All that year Henry was ill on and off: when his leg broke out he had to rest; restored, he rose from bed to resume the day's activities until it flared again. That he lasted so long must be attributed to a spirit that refused to accept defeat, and to his doctor's skills. He set off for his customary progress in September, only this time he spared himself the fatigue of receiving many addresses and deputations, and stayed at manor houses and country seats far removed from towns.

He went first to the only palace he ever built, for he was not a builder in the sense that Wolsey was. This was a favourite resort of his which he called None-Such, and he was right. No such edifice has ever been erected like it, for it sprang from his fertile brain, larger and more colourful than any other, too long for its height until a commandingly tall tower was added at either end, all turrets, cupolas and domes. The ground floor alone was built of stone; the lofty storeys above were constructed of timber and plaster. The plaster was painted with pictures that told a story, the timber covered with lead and gilded. When the sun shone on this fantastic building, it was a sight worthy of its royal builder's eye.

On his return he moved from castle to palace and back to castle. He suffered from winter colds but still gave audiences to foreign ambassadors, his ministers and Chancellor, still hunted from a butt and persisted each day in taking outdoor exercise. He had to be assisted to mount his horse, and indoors was carried from room to room up and down stairs in a chair. Sometimes he would dress to go to mass or into the palace gardens, and instead sat brooding where he was. The ulcers on his legs had spread and had to be cauterized, an extreme and painful treatment, yet he transacted state business up to the day before he died.

The scales between the two factions in his Council which he kept balanced as he thought fit weighed towards the Reformers: this indicated the regency council he would nominate in his will to act for his son. It was his strength that he kept them fairly equal; preponderance one way or another was dangerous and he was far too astute to commit himself to either party. That autumn he discussed with Cranmer ways and means of turning the mass into a communion service.

Suddenly the balance was destroyed. Norfolk and his mountebank son Surrey were both sent to the Tower, the father made to suffer for the son, who had quartered his coat-of-arms with the royal arms and asked who had more right to be Protector when the King died than his father.

The royal prerogative was challenged. The Norfolks with their blue blood could well cause trouble during Edward's minority when his father was no longer there to keep them in their place. Henry had shown in the past his unanswerable method of dealing with possible pretenders, and he was taking no chances where his son was concerned.

Silent crowds watched the poet Surrey go to his death, he who had threatened the inheritance of their rightful little Prince whose reign was to inaugurate a golden world. His father's execution was stayed only because the King who ordered it died before it could be carried out.

What was he thinking as he lay in Wolsey's palace of Whitehall? He had so much to remember, yet it is not the large scenes that crowd the mind as the self withdraws, but little things, fugitive as the few notes of a full score.

Did he remember the pounding of his horse's hoofs as he chased the French in the Battle of the Spurs? These were the days he had breath to blow the captain's whistle on one of his new ships until it sounded like a trumpet. Did bugle notes reach him from a little hill when his sun was high in the heavens? It was winter now, January 1547, when there was no meridian, and he was old, in the fifty-fifth year of his age and the thirty-eighth of his reign.

He had always hated to hear of death, and his doctors dare not tell him because his own Act of Parliament made it treason to prophesy the King's demise. It was his chief gentleman of the chamber who boldly told him what case he was in that he might prepare himself for the end. His King demanded what judge had sent him to cast this sentence upon him, to which Sir Anthony Denny replied, "Your Grace's physicians."

He was asked if he would like to speak to any of his bishops but he said, "I will see no one but Cranmer, but not him as yet. Let me repose a little, and as I find myself, so shall I determine."

When he woke he felt the feebleness of death upon him and told Denny to send for Cranmer. The Archbishop arrived after midnight to find the King unable to speak. He saw he was recognized, for his master stretched out his hand to him and would not let his go. Cranmer spoke comfortably to him, urging him to give some sign by eye or hand that he put his trust in God through Jesus Christ. With his last strength, Henry wrung his Archbishop's hand hard.

A Chronology of Henry VIII

1485	Accession of Henry VII.
	Birth of Katherine of Aragon.
1491	Birth of Henry.
1501	Marriage of Katherine of Aragon and Arthur, Prince of Wales, Henry's brother.
1502	Death of Arthur.
1503	Marriage of Margaret, Henry's sister, to James IV of Scotland.
1509	Death of Henry VII.
	Marriage of Henry to Katherine of Aragon.
	Coronation of Henry.
1513	Battle of the Spurs.
	Battle of Flodden.
1514	Marriage of Mary, Henry's sister, to Louis XII.
1515	Marriage of Mary, Henry's sister, to Charles Brandon, Duke of Suffolk.
1516	Birth of Mary, daughter of Henry and Katherine of Aragon.
1519	Birth of Henry Fitzroy, illegitimate son of Henry and Elizabeth Blount.
1520	Field of Cloth of Gold.
1530	Death of Wolsey.

1533	Marriage of Henry to Anne Boleyn.

1533   Marriage of Henry to Anne Boleyn.
Death of Mary, Henry's sister.
Birth of Elizabeth, daughter of Henry and Anne Boleyn.

1536   Death of Katherine of Aragon.
Execution of Anne Boleyn.
Marriage of Henry to Jane Seymour.

1537   Birth of Edward (later Edward VI), son of Henry and Jane Seymour.
Death of Jane Seymour.

1540   Marriage of Henry to Anne of Cleves.

1540   Marriage of Henry to Katherine Howard.

1541   Death of Margaret, Henry's sister.

1542   Battle of Solway Moss.
Execution of Katherine Howard.

1543   Marriage of Henry to Katherine Parr.

1547   Death of Henry.

INDEX

250

available wherever paperbacks are sold ...

CATHERINE, THE QUEEN
by Mary M. Luke

The millions of readers of *Mary Queen of Scots,* and viewers of CBS-TV's phenomenally popular series, "The Six Wives of Henry VIII," will be even more enchanted by this vibrant, richly detailed biography of Catherine of Aragon, first wife of Henry VIII of England—the woman who wed two English princes; who heard her marriage to Henry proclaimed an offense to God; who survived pregnancy after pregnancy without producing the son who would have secured her place in Henry's heart and at his court; and who won and held the allegiance of the English people—even when she could not hold their King.

☐ (68-743, $1.50)

You will also enjoy ...

☐ **A CROWN FOR ELIZABETH**
   by Mary M. Luke   (68-787, $1.50)

MORE GREAT BOOKS
FROM THE PAGES OF HISTORY!